Olympic Winners

Reading Activities for Schools and Libraries

Marcia Lund

Alleyside® Press

Fort Atkinson, Wisconsin

For Joseph Karl Swiggum, my son.

Acknowledgements
I am grateful for the editing expertise of Don Sager and Nancy Wilcox.
A special thanks to Frank Neu for the brilliantly colored cover. Thanks
to Mary Holbrook for all the hours she spent typing. Thanks to the students (4/5–7/8 units) in my EAGLE physical education classes for helping me decide which sports to include.

Thanks to my parents, family, and friends for supporting me and
bringing me meals when I was too busy to cook. Special thanks to
my brother, Dave for helping me develop my love for sports.
Without that, this book would not have been possible.

Published by Alleyside Press, an imprint of Highsmith Press LLC
Highsmith Press
W5527 Highway 106
P.O. Box 800
Fort Atkinson, Wisconsin 53538-0800
1-800-558-2110

© Marcia Lund , 1996
Cover design: Frank Neu

The paper used in this publication meets the minimum requirements of
American National Standard for Information Science — Permanence of Paper for
Printed Library Material. ANSI/NISO Z39.48-1992.

Contents

Olympic Motto

Swifter, Higher, Stronger

Olympic Creed

The most important thing in the Olympic Games is not to win but to take part, just as the most important thing in life is not the triumph, but the struggle. The essential thing is not to have conquered but to have fought well.

Introduction

Olympic Winners emerged as a creation from some of my favorite passions; writing, teaching, and sports. Olympic athletes have fascinated me ever since I watched Olga Korbut on television in 1972 as a young girl. Like thousands of other viewers, I was electrified by the grace and beauty of the sport. It seemed to be more than physical movements and outstanding execution.

Olympic athletes have a desire that spills over into every effort they make. It is too difficult to name the exact traits that make them different, but it must include qualities such as fierce determination, courage, a flair for creativity, discipline, concentration, risk, humility, and spontaneity. Most of all, an immeasurable amount of spirit carries these athletes through any imaginable ordeal. Perhaps this spirit and added excitement is connected to the four year intervals between each of the summer Olympic Games. Would they have the same degree of intensity if they were scheduled every year? At any rate, the event continues to place Olympic athletes in a category of their own, transcending the glory of professional leagues to a new dimension.

The athletes may draw us to the Olympics, but it is the events which draw the athletes there. This book offers a look at some of those events and celebrated athletes. Included are historical backgrounds of twenty-four summer Olympic events, brief profiles of significant athletes or participating teams in each of the events, activities for teachers to use in a language arts (reading, writing, or drama) classroom, and an annotated bibliography. The order of the events is arranged to reflect their historical place in the Games.

In general, the "Activities and Discussion" sections offer three levels of activities, the first for fourth and fifth grade students; the second for fifth and sixth graders; and the third for seventh and eighth grade students. One of the added features in the cycling section is an interview with Connie Carpenter-Phinney, gold medalist in the road race in 1984.

It is my hope, as a teacher, to spark curiosity in students about the Olympic events and athletes. Teaching requires a balance of knowledge, enthusiasm, and careful attention to children. As Madeleine L'Engle once said about teaching children, "What a teacher or librarian or parent can do, in working with children, is to give the flame enough oxygen so that it can burn. As far as I'm concerned, this providing of oxygen is one of the noblest of all vocations."[1]

Notes

1. L'Engle, *A Circle of Quiet*, New York: HarperCollins, 1984, p. 46.

Ancient Olympic Games

The Olympic Games originated nearly 3,000 years ago, but there was a period when they were not observed. The Modern Olympic Games were revived in 1896, with the 100th anniversary celebration taking place during the summer games in Atlanta.

The ancient games started as a festival to honor Hercules, the son of Zeus. As in the modern Olympics, the festival took place every four years. Accounts indicate that up to 40,000 people gathered at Olympia, near Altis, to observe these games.

The events included foot races and the pentathlon (running, jumping, the discus, wrestling, and the javelin). Instead of winning gold, silver, and bronze medals, the treasured prize was an olive wreath placed on the athlete's head like a crown. The winners often became famous. Artists created statues in their likenesses. They ate free meals for months and were exempt from paying taxes for life.

The spirit of the ancient games changed when professionals were allowed to compete. They were drawn into the competition with cash offers and bribes. When the Macedonians conquered the territory near Mount Olympus, the ancient games ceased. The Romans reintroduced the competition, but it resembled a violent and cruel form of entertainment. Emperor Theodosius stamped out the tradition completely, deeming it pagan and forbidden.

The torch burns today, not for cash advances or acclaim, but for the love of the sport.

Marathon Running

The word "*marathon*" comes from the sea town Marathon, Greece. In 490 B.C., a lone messenger ran from Marathon to Athens to announce the victory of 7,000 Greek warriors over 20,000 Persians. The town was approximately 40 kilometers (twenty-four miles) from Athens. After he reached the city he called out "Nenikikamen" ("We are victorious!"), then he crumbled to the ground and died.

In the 1908 Olympics held in London, the distance for the marathon race became official. King Edward VII and Queen Alexandra planned a birthday party for one of their grandchildren on the Windsor Castle lawn. As entertainment, they asked the Olympic officials if the marathon could begin at Windsor Castle. The officials agreed. The distance from Windsor to London's White City Stadium was 26 miles 385 yards. To this day, the marathon distance remains the same.

In the first modern Olympics held in Athens, Spiridon Louis of Greece won the gold medal in the marathon. Prince George and Prince Constantine were so pleased that a Greek athlete led the race, they ran to either side of Louis and finished the race by his side.

Marathon Training

World-class marathon runners work on running at a consistent pace throughout the race, rather than adjusting to the pace of the other runners. A leader of the pack at the ten-mile or twenty-mile mark may not even finish the race or be in the top ten finishers. Conditioning is the key in this race. Runners may have difficulties with dehydration, blisters, or heat exhaustion. It is run on paved streets with hills or valleys. Many of the top marathon runners complete the distance within two hours and eight minutes.

Famous Marathon Runners in Olympic History

Spiridon Louis Greece; Athens, 1896 (Time: 2:58:50).
Louis won the first marathon in the modern Olympic Games.

Dorando Pietri Italy; London, 1908 (Disqualified).
A 22-year-old candy maker from Italy, Dorando Pietri gave spectators one of the most thrilling performances in Olympic history. Coming into the final stretch, Pietri and Charles Hefferon from South Africa battled for first place. Of the 56 marathon runners, twenty-three had dropped out due to the mugginess and hot weather. As Pietri entered the stadium just ahead of Hefferon he turned the wrong way. Trackside officials ran to his aid steering him in the right direction. He stumbled and fell, rose, stumbled and fell to the ground again. Five times he fell, but each time he picked himself up and continued the race. Determined to finish, he staggered to the finish line. Just before he stepped over the line, an official reached

out to help him across the line. Officials carried him off the field on a stretcher to receive medical assistance. Meanwhile, the Italian flag was hoisted on the victory pole to celebrate Pietri's finish. Johnny Hayes, an American finished second after Pietri. Disturbed by the assistance Pietri received from the trackside officials, he protested the first place finish. Pietri was disqualified and Hayes became the gold medalist. Even though Pietri lost the gold medal, he became an international celebrity for his demonstration of perseverance and courage.

Sohn Kee-Chung Korea; Berlin, 1936 (Time: 2:29:19).
Chung competed in the Berlin Olympics wearing the rising sun symbol of the Japanese flag. At that time Japan occupied Korea. When Sohn Kee-Chung won the gold medal, he bowed his head during the Japanese national anthem. Fifty-two years later the glory of his marathon victory became a reality in his home country. At the age of 76, Sohn Kee Chung carried the torch to light the Olympic flame for the 1988 Summer Olympics in Seoul, Korea.

Abebe Bikila Ethiopia; Rome, 1960; Tokyo, 1964 (Time: 2:12:11).
Bikila ran the entire marathon in Rome barefoot and won the gold medal. He repeated the first place finish in Tokyo with shoes.

Frank Shorter United States; Munich, 1972; Montreal, 1976 (Time: 2:12:19).
Shorter won the gold medal in 1972 and the silver in 1976. His popularity spread throughout the United States, sparking a new interest in long distance running.

Joan Benoit United States, 1984 Los Angeles (Time: 2:24:52).
After the 1928 Amsterdam Games when several women collapsed at the 800-meter run finish line, women were not allowed to compete in long distance running events. Fifty-six years later, Benoit won the gold in the marathon.

Further Reading

Aaseng, Nathan. *World-Class Marathoners*. Minneapolis, MN: Lerner Publications Co., 1982. 80 pp. Provides background on the history of the marathon and seven great marathon runners. Reading level: 2nd–6th grade.

Littlefield, Bill. Paintings by Bernie Fuchs. *Champions: Stories of Ten Remarkable Athletes*. Boston, MA: Little, Brown and Co., 1993. 132 pp. Detailed accounts of ten athletes who have demonstrated tremendous courage and will power to excel. Beautifully illustrated. Reading level: 4th–8th grade.

Paulsen, Gary. *Woodsong*. New York, NY: Puffin Books, 1990. 132 pp. True story about the author's challenge racing in the Iditarod in Alaska. An ALA Best Book for Young Adults. Reading level: 5th–8th grade.

Dolan, Ellen M. *Susan Butcher and the Iditarod Trail*. New York, NY: Walker Publishing Co., 1993. 103 pp. Fascinating account and history of the Iditarod and Susan Butcher's experiences racing. Photos and maps included. Reading level: 4th–8th grade.

Marathon Running Activities and Discussion Questions

1. Read aloud the chapter on Susan Butcher in the book *Champions* by Bill Littlefield. In small groups of three or four students, pick one of the following activities to prepare and present to the class:

   - Study the history of the Iditarod and draw a map of the 1100 mile course from Anchorage to Nome Alaska.

   - Read about Siberian Huskies and why they are the most common breed of dogs used in the Iditarod. Do breeders like to breed other species with Huskies to change the Husky stock? What other breeds might be chosen?

   - What kind of training does Susan Butcher have to do to compete in the Iditarod? Give examples.

   - Why might the Iditarod be called one of the ultimate tests of endurance. Name other sports besides marathon running and sled dog racing that test an athlete's endurance.

2. As a class read the book *Woodsong* by Gary Paulsen, a true story about the grueling Iditarod race.

3. Research the following women. What conclusions or patterns can you discover?

Marilyn Bell	Irene van der Laan
Cindy Nicholas	Shelley Taylor
Julie Ridge	Gertrude Ederle
Florence Chadwick	

4. Debate the following statements using evidence from the preceding activities or your own knowledge to back up your opinions:

   In most cases, women are better than men at endurance sports because they have more body fat.

   Men are stronger and faster than women because they have twenty percent more muscle.

Learning Objectives: To introduce students to many different endurance sports and champions. To compare and contrast men's and women's physical capabilities in endurance sports.

Answer to question 3.: In most cases, women are better than men at endurance sports because they have more body fat. Men are stronger and faster than women because they have 20% more muscle.

Running – Sprints

Sprints
100-meter dash
200-meter dash
Relays

The origins of sprinting in the Olympics date back to 776 B.C. when a sprinter named Coroebus won a footrace of 630 ft. (193m), equivalent to the length of the stadium. According to the records of that day, the footrace was the *only* event of the Games. Hundreds of years later, about A.D.394, the Olympic Games were discontinued because they were thought to be pagan. In the 1100s and late 1800s England started to formalize the competition in track and field. The first college track meet between Oxford and Cambridge took place in 1864. The English created running tracks from turnpike roads and horse racing tracks. By 1896, they claimed to have the most running tracks in Europe. An Englishman designed the track used in Athens for the first modern Olympics.

Women could not compete in any track and field events until 1928.

Rules of Sprinting

Each individual running a sprint must start in one of eight lanes. The 100-meter dash is a straightaway, the 200-meter has a slight curving turn on the track. Most sprints use starting blocks at the beginning of the race. The starter gives two commands, "On your marks" and "Set" before he fires a starting pistol. If there is a false start, the runner is given a warning. Two false starts disqualify the sprinter. At the finish line, the torso must cross an imaginary line running vertically from the finish line. Electronic timing devices and photos of the finish help judges decide the winner when it is too close for the eye to call.

Four phases of the short sprint:

Start In a 100-meter sprint an explosive start is critical to the entire race. The torso should stay horizontal at the start.

Acceleration The knees stretch out, arms pump, and the body gradually moves upright.

Stride After making the transition from the crouched posture, the runner races smoothly and on the balls of his feet.

Finish Before the racer reaches the tape, he shortens the length of his steps and leans forward to hit the tape with his torso.

Famous Sprinters in Olympic History

Jesse Owens United States; Berlin, 1936.
Owens became an international star during the Berlin Games winning four gold medals in the 100-meter run, 200-meter, 4x100 relay (4 laps of 100-meters), and long jump. When Owens won these gold medals, Hitler, the master of ceremonies, did not congratulate him or shake his hand as he did with other gold medal winners. Hitler believed that Germans were superior to all other races and that African-

Americans were inferior. Despite this affront, Owens proved himself to be the fastest human being in the world. In 1951 Jesse Owens returned to Berlin. During the half time of a Harlem Globetrotters game, he took a victory lap around the Olympic Stadium where he had run the 100-meter dash in 1936. After the lap, Ernst Reuter, the mayor of West Berlin, greeted him and shook both his hands.

Wilma Rudolph United States; Melbourne, 1956; Rome, 1960.
Rudolph won a bronze medal in the 4x100 relay team in Melbourne and three gold medals in the 100-meter dash, 200-meter and 4x100 relay in Rome.

Rudolph overcame tremendous obstacles to compete and win these Olympic gold medals. She was the twentieth of twenty-two children in her family. She was born weighing only four pounds. At age four she became ill with pneumonia and scarlet fever; the result of these illnesses left her with a crippled leg. As a girl she wore braces on her legs and continued to receive treatment until the age of twelve. Despite these challenges she loved to play basketball and other sports, and four years after getting rid of her braces, she qualified for the Olympic Games in Melbourne at age sixteen. Two years later, Rudolph became pregnant, just weeks after graduating from high school. With the support of her coaches and parents she continued her education at Tennessee State and competed in the Olympics again in 1960.

Carl Lewis United States; Los Angeles, 1984; Seoul, 1988; Barcelona, 1992.
Carl Lewis won four gold medals in Los Angeles in the 100-meter sprint, 200-meter sprint, 4x100 relay and long jump; two gold medals in Seoul in the 100-meter and long jump; adding a silver in the 200-meter; and two gold medals in Barcelona for the long jump and 4x100 relay team. Interestingly Carl Lewis received medals in the same track events as Jesse Owens, who he viewed as his inspiration. Unlike Owens, Lewis was able to compete in three Olympic Games.

When asked how he wanted to be remembered, Lewis replied, "I hope I can just be remembered as someone who inspired people and led them to do things they never thought they could do."[1]

Irena Szewinska Poland; Tokyo, 1964; Mexico City, 1968; Munich, 1972; Montreal, 1976.
Szewinska is known as the queen of the track in Poland, and she is another example of superb conditioning and endurance achieved over many years of training. When she was eighteen, she won a gold in the 4x100 relay, and two silvers in the 200-meter sprints and the long jump. In 1968 she won a gold in the 200-meter and a bronze in the 100-meter. She injured her ankle between the Games in 1968 and 1972. This injury kept her from training, as did a pregnancy with her son Andrej. She competed again in 1976 and won a bronze in the 200-meter. After running the 100-meter and 200-meter sprints, she decided to train for the 400-meter with her husbands help. Two years later she broke the world record for the 400-meter with a time under 50 seconds. Competing in her fourth Olympics, Szewinska barely qualified for the finals in the 400-meter, but she persevered and won the gold.

She competed in the Olympic Games from the age of eighteen until she was 30. Even though Irena Szewinska's name may not be as well known as Babe Didrickson or Jackie Joyner-Kersee, she has demonstrated tremendous discipline, commitment and devotion to achieving her goals.

Further Reading

Aaseng, Nathan. *Florence Griffith Joyner*. Minneapolis, MN: Lerner Publications, 1989. 60 pp. Highlights the life of an outstanding sprinter in the 100-meter, 200-meter, and 4x100 relay. Reading level: 4th–8th grade.

Koral, April. *Florence Griffith Joyner*. New York: Franklin Watts, 1992. 64 pp. Spotlights the Olympic superstar after her gold medal victories in the Seoul Olympics in 1988. Reading level: 3rd–6th grade.

Owens, Jesse and Paul G. Neimark. *The Jesse Owens Story*. New York: G.P. Putnam's Sons, 1970. 109 pp. Written in the first person, this is the remarkable story of how Owens surmounted tremendous obstacles to be the top athlete in the world. Reading level: 3rd–6th grade.

Rennert, Rick. *Jesse Owens*. New York: Chelsea Juniors, 1992. 79 pp. Biography on one of the greatest sprinters in Olympic history. Reading level: 3rd–6th grade.

Notes:
1. Greenspan, Bud. *100 Greatest Moments in Olympic History*. Los Angeles: General Publishing, 1995. p. 157.

Sprinters Activities and Discussion Questions

100-meter dash 200-meter dash Relays

1. Read a biography or sports profile on Jesse Owens, Wilma Rudolph, Carl Lewis, or Florence Griffith Joyner. Write a letter as if you are one of these famous personalities and you are giving encouragement to perform a skill, enter a competition or develop confidence in a sport.

2. Using a sports almanac or Olympic fact book plot the times of at least ten winners of the 100- and 200-meter races for men and women. Make a visual chart illustrating the differences in times.

3. One of the controversies of the 1936 Berlin Games was the strong, anti-Semitic and anti-Black statements and pro-German propaganda. In a poll held in the United States at the time, 57% of the American public voted in favor of a boycott.

    After researching the controversies surrounding the Nazis and the propaganda Hitler spread throughout Germany, write an essay on whether or not you would vote to boycott or attend the 1936 Games in Berlin. Check your library for information on the 1980 Olympics, which were boycotted by the United States. Why did this occur?

Learning Objectives: To read about some of the fastest men and women in the history of running. To plot times of gold medal winners from different decades. To write an essay about the controversies in 1936 Games held in Berlin.

Decathlon

Decathlon Events (men only)

First Day
100-meter sprint
Long jump
Shot put
High jump
400-meter sprint

Second Day
110-meter high hurdles
Discus throw
Pole vault
Javelin throw
1,500-meter run

The combination of throwing, running, and jumping events were part of the ancient Olympic Games in 708 B.C. At that time participants competed in only five events: discus, running, wrestling, javelin, and long jump. The modern Olympics offered the decathlon for the first time in 1904 in St. Louis. Even though decathlon athletes may not be the top finishers in one event, they are often considered the greatest athletes for their versatility and stamina. At times the athletes must compete for more than twelve hours in one day. Typically, the competitors race or participate in a field event and have a 30-minute break between each event. The entire decathlon event lasts only two days.

Strategy

Placing first, second, or third in an event is not the primary concern in a decathlon. Scoring the most points based on a formula of time and distance sets the strategic course for the athletes. Bruce Jenner won only two out of ten events outright, but he won the gold and broke the world record in the decathlon scoring 8,618 points.

Famous Decathloners in Olympic History

Jim Thorpe United States; Stockholm, 1912.
King Gustav V, the master of ceremonies at the 1912 Games in Stockholm proclaimed that Jim Thorpe was the greatest athlete in the world. He had won the gold medal in the decathlon and the pentathlon. In the decathlon, Thorpe scored 700 points more than the second place finisher.

Thorpe suffered many losses as a boy. His twin brother died when he was only eight, he lost his mother when he was twelve and then his father died three years later. Despite these hardships, Thorpe's achievements fulfilled the vision of his mother when she gave him his American Indian name, Wa-Tho-Huck, meaning "Bright Path."

Thorpe was active in football, basketball, and baseball, and this led him to participate in the Olympics. During a college football game for Carlisle against Army in 1911, Thorpe ran 92 yards for a touchdown. Because of a penalty on the play, the touchdown did not count. On the next play, however, Thorpe repeated the feat, running 97 yards this time and scoring a touchdown.

Six months after the summer Games in 1912, a story was leaked to the newspapers saying Thorpe had accepted $25 per week to play semi-professional baseball before his appearance in the Olympics. Since professional athletes were excluded from competing in the Olympics, the Amateur Athletic Union decided to strip Thorpe of his gold medals and erase his name from the record books.

Thorpe went on to play major league baseball with the New York Giants and later for the Cincinnati Reds. He played professional football until the Depression in 1929.

Thirty-eight years after Thorpe's participation in the Olympics, sportswriters from the Associated Press voted Jim Thorpe the greatest athlete in the first 50 years of the twentieth century. Seventy years after Thorpe won the pentathlon and decathlon, the International Olympic Committee reinstated him as the gold medalist in 1912. His medals were given to his children in 1983.

Robert Mathias United States; London, 1948; Helsinki, 1952.

At the age of seventeen, Mathias was one of the youngest decathlon athletes in Olympic history. He began training only months before the London Games. He fouled in the shot put event because of his inexperience, but his fierce determination and dedication gave him the first place victory. The people from his community of 12,000 were so elated when they heard the news of his victory, they crowded the streets and closed businesses. So many went to greet him at the airport that Mathias' airplane was delayed to clear the runway of people.

In 1952 Mathias repeated his first place finish, winning by a margin of 632 points.

Francis "Daley" Thompson Great Britain; Montreal, 1976; Moscow, 1980; Los Angeles, 1984.

Daley competed in the decathlon in Montreal finishing 18th. By 1980, he had trained hard and knew his technique and stamina had improved. He won the gold in Moscow and again four years later in Los Angeles.

Further Reading

Bortstein, Larry. *After Olympic Glory: The Lives of Ten Outstanding Medalists*. New York: Fredrick Warne, 1978. 185 pp. Features stories about ten Olympic champions such as Bob Mathias, Micki King, and Bill Bradley and their pursuits after the Olympic victories. Reading level: 5th–10th grade.

Lipsyte, Robert. *Jim Thorpe: 20th Century Jock*. New York: HarperCollins Publishers, 1993. 103 pp. Outstanding biography on one of the greatest athletes in Olympic history. Reading level: 4th–6th grade.

Schoor, Gene. *The Jim Thorpe Story*. New York: Julian Messner, 1967. 187 pp. Known for his record-breaking performances in football, baseball, and track and field events in the Olympics, Jim Thorpe's achievements are presented in this well-written and popular book. Reading level: 5th–8th grade.

Matthews, Peter. *Guinness Track and Field Athletics*. Great Britain: Guinness, 1986. 175 pp. Essentially a record book for track and field events, but it also features profiles on several athletes from around the world. Reading level: 3rd grade–Adult.

Decathlon Activities and Discussion Questions

1. Field Day Extravaganza – After reading about the decathlon and the events, work with a partner to plan a field day including ten events. Try to make the events suitable for your age group. For example, if you are going to include hurdles, make sure the hurdles are a comfortable height. Try to invent new twists to running races or relays. Here are a few examples:

   Banana Relay: In an oval track, have four people stand equally apart. When the teacher says, "Go" the racers follow the track passing a banana instead of a baton.

   50-yard Mash: Racers run 50-yards then pop a balloon and run back to the finish line.

2. Metric Measurements – The metric system of measurement is used all around the world. However, the United States has not converted to it. Read about the metric system in an encyclopedia. What are the benefits of the metric system? What are the disadvantages? Do you think the United States should convert? When you buy a large container of soda, is it a liter size or a half gallon? Why do you think it might be difficult to switch to the metric system?

   What do the following terms mean? What are the dimensions in U.S. measurements?

centimeter	decimeter	meter
dekameter	kilometer	centiliter
deciliter	liter	kiloliter

3. When Jim Thorpe was accused of violating the codes of the Amateur Athletic Union, Thorpe's response was "I did not play for the money, I played because I liked baseball." Read about the predicament Thorpe experienced in the 1912 Olympics. Imagine you are Jim Thorpe and the AAU wants to take away the two gold medals you earned in the pentathlon and the decathlon. How will you convince them they have made a mistake?

Learning Objectives: To think of creative events for a field day. To discuss the metric system and talk about the advantages and disadvantages of the metric system. To research a controversial decision in Olympic history.

LONG JUMP

Part of the Olympics since the first competition in 1896, the men's long jump has been dominated by Americans in all but two years. The women's competition did not begin until 1948. The German, Soviet, and Romanian women have won medals in many of the Olympics since that time.

Four phases of the long jump:

Approach Jumpers sprint down a runway to pick up speed for the take-off.

Take-off Like a bird or an airplane, the jumper strives to gain as much height as possible without losing speed from the approach. One foot hits the take-off board, heel first, the other foot swings forward and up in the air.

Flight While in the air, jumpers may have different styles of jumping. One might try *sailing*—a style in which the jumpers legs are held together in a sitting position. *Hanging* looks as if one leg is weighted down and sweeps forward during the flight. The *hitch-kick* style appears as if the jumper is running in mid-air, pumping his legs to reach the greatest distance.

Landing With the body weight shifting forward, legs extended, arms forward, the jumper lands and falls either forward or sideways after the landing. If he falls backwards the measurement is taken from the point where his hands or back touch the sand.

Strategy

The combination of speed and precise timing at the take-off gives the jumper the added edge in competition. Fouls can be quite common. Both Jesse Owens and Bob Beamon relied on advice from other long jumpers to prevent fouling. Both won the gold medal after listening to the advice. Each jumper is allowed three qualifying jumps, three jumps in the final competition, and three jumps in the medal round.

Famous Long Jumpers In Olympic History

<u>Jesse Owens</u> United States; Berlin, 1936 (26' 5½"[8.06m]).
Owens broke the Olympic record in a riveting competition against Luz Long, the German favorite. In the year before the Berlin Games, Owens broke the world record with a jump of 26' 8¼". This record remained unbroken for 25 years.

Dimensions of the Landing Pit

The landing pit itself is 32' 9" long.

Take-off board is 4' long and 7¾" wide.

Bob Beamon United States; Mexico City, 1968 (29' 2½" [8.90m]).

One of the most astonishing achievements in the history of the Olympics occurred in Mexico City in 1968. Bob Beamon, a twenty-two-year-old from New York City participated in the men's long jump competition. At a height of 6'3" and weighing 160 lbs., Beamon's lanky and light frame allowed him to leap with tremendous height and distance. However, his inconsistency hurt his overall performance. He often overstepped the take-off board and fouled.

In the qualifying round, Beamon fouled on his first two attempts. He had only one more try to reach the finals. Ralph Boston, Beamon's teammate suggested that he draw a special foul line in front of the official one. Beamon followed this advice and qualified.

In the final round on the very first jump, Beamon soared through the air and landed much further than any of the other jumpers. He realized it was a phenomenal jump, but could not estimate the extent of his achievement. In fact, the judges also had a difficult time measuring the jump, because it was longer than the electronic measuring device was set to measure. The judges found an old cloth tape measure and announced the distance as 8.90 meters. When this was converted to feet and inches, Beamon heard it and fell to his knees. He had just broken the world record by 21¾ inches! He collapsed from the shock and suffered a cataleptic seizure.

No other competitor came close to Beamon's record during that year. The silver medalist jumped 26'10". For twenty-three years Beamon held the world record, never coming within two feet of his own record in the years that followed. In 1991 at the World Championships in Tokyo, Mike Powell, broke Beamon's record with a jump of 29' 4½".

Carl Lewis United States; Los Angeles, 1984; Seoul, 1988; Barcelona, 1992
(Best leap: 29' 1¼").

Lewis won gold medals in the long jump in three Olympic Games.

Jackie Joyner-Kersee United States; Seoul, 1988; Barcelona, 1992 (7.40m).

Joyner-Kersee holds the Olympic record in long jump. She won the gold in 1988 and the bronze in 1992.

Further Reading:

Adler, David A. Illustrated by Robert Casilla. *A Picture Book of Jesse Owens*. New York: Holiday House, 1992. 29 pp. Highlights the important events in Jesse Owens' life. Reading level: 1st–4th grade.

Gentry, Tony. *Jesse Owens*. New York: Chelsea House Publishers, 1990. 110 pp. Detailed chapters on the 1936 Berlin Olympics and Jesse Owen's influence on African Americans after his victories. Reading level: 6th–8th grade.

Long Jump Activities and Discussion Questions

1. Using an updated *Guinness Book of Olympic Records* or *Sports Almanac*, make a chart of the gold medal jumps for men and women in the Olympic Games since 1896. You may want to use posterboard or ask a computer teacher to help you set up a chart on a computer. Students may wish to work in groups of three or four. How common is it for long jumpers like Bob Beamon to beat a previous gold medal winner by over twenty-one inches?

2. Read a biography on Jesse Owens, and then study the following related topics through encyclopedias or other books:
   Slavery (Jesse Owens' grandparents were slaves.)
   Sharecroppers (Owens' parents were sharecroppers.)
   Hitler and Nazism
   Hitler's Views about the Jewish people and African Americans

3. After Jesse Owens returned from the 1936 Olympics, Americans celebrated his victories with a parade and formal events. However, his fame did not translate into fortune until many years later. How much money an Olympic athlete makes after winning a gold medal was partially dependent on the time period in which he or she lived and how willing the athlete was to sign contracts for commercials. Find out how difficult or easy it was for the following Olympic athletes to make money after their Olympic appearances. Be sure to write down the year they competed in the Olympics and give details on how they earned money following their victories.

Jesse Owens	Mark Spitz
Jim Thorp	Bruce Jenner
Johnny Weissmuller	Eric Heiden
Babe Didrikson	Mary Lou Retton
Sonja Henie	Dorothy Hamill

Learning Objectives: To demonstrate the difference between "ordinary" (for Olympic athletes) improvements in Olympic records and "extraordinary" results. To introduce the historical background of a great man. To highlight and think about the role of commercialism in the Olympics.

Heptathlon

The ancient Greeks combined throwing events with running and jumping events when they held their first pentathlon in 708 B.C. Along with running races, they included wrestling, javelin, discus throws, and long jump. Women did not compete in the pentathlon until 1964. In 1980, two more events were added to the pentathlon to create the heptathlon.

Athletes participating in the heptathlon attempt to score the highest number of points in seven different events over a two-day period. The International Amateur Athletic Federation provides a chart that awards each athlete a set number of points based on a formula involving time and distance. If an athlete misses one event, she is eliminated from the competition. The heptathlon tests one's ability to be versatile, using a variety of muscles, and one's stamina and ability to withstand many trials of endurance over two days. Between events there is only a 30 minute rest period. Some believe the heptathlon is the ultimate test of the greatest athlete.

Events in the Heptathlon

First Day
200-meter dash
100-meter hurdles
High jump
Shot put

Second Day
Long jump
Javelin throw
800-meter run

Strategy

The winners of the heptathlon may not be the winners of every event. The best approach for this competition is placing well in as many events as possible. Individual times and distances for throwing or jumping make the difference in scoring.

Famous Women Competitors in the Pentathlon and Heptathlon

Nadezhda Tkachenko Soviet Union; Moscow, 1980 (5083 pts).
Tkachenko won the gold in Moscow and broke the world record in the pentathlon. Her teammate Olga Rukavishnikova held the world record for a mere four-tenths of a second until Tkachenko beat her.

Mary Peters Great Britain; Tokyo, 1964; Mexico City, 1968; Munich, 1972 (4801 pts).
After finishing fourth in the 1964 pentathlon and ninth in 1968, Peters boosted her performance to win the gold in 1972 with 4801 points. She was 33-years-old at the time.

Jackie Joyner-Kersee United States; Los Angeles, 1984; Seoul, 1988; Barcelona, 1992 (7,291 pts).
Jackie Joyner-Kersee holds the world record in the heptathlon despite the fact that she suffers from exercise-induced asthma. Nothing seems to hold her back. It almost seems as if the odds were against her from the beginning. Born of teenage parents in East St. Louis, a poverty-stricken community, Joyner-Kersee made a pact with her brother to reach for her dreams. Inspired by watching the 1976 Olympics on television, she decided to set her sights toward becoming an Olympic athlete herself. At the age of fourteen she won the first of four pentathlon championships.

Recruited by UCLA to play basketball, she soon found herself working toward becoming a heptathlete under the guidance of her coach, (and later husband) Bob Kersee. In 1984, Joyner Kersee missed winning the gold by only six hundredths of a second in the 800-meter run. In 1986, she broke the world record. She received the Sullivan Award and the Jesse Owens Award for her tremendous achievements. In 1988, she won the gold medal in the heptathlon and the long jump competition. In 1992, she won the gold for the second time in the heptathlon, and a bronze in the long jump. Keeping it in the family, her brother, Al Joyner, won a gold in the triple jump in the 1984 Olympics.

In 1996 at Atlanta, Joyner-Kersee will compete again at age 34. No one in Olympic history has ever won a multi-event at age 34, but Joyner-Kersee has previously set many Olympic records. During one, she said "That's the ultimate challenge—to do something nobody has been able to do,... I would love that."[1]

Further Reading

Goldstein, Margaret J. and Jennifer Larson. *Jackie Joyner Kersee*. Minneapolis, MN: Lerner Publications. 1994. 56 pp. Presents a biographical history of Kersee's life and involvement in the Olympics. Reading level: 4th–8th grade.

Greenspan, Bud. *100 Greatest Moments in Olympic History*. Los Angeles: General Publ., 1995. 224 pp. Outstanding biographical profiles of Olympic athletes and teams. Reading level: 4th grade–Adult.

Notes
1. Nelson, Rebecca and Marie J. Mackee. *The Olympic Factbook*. Detroit, MI: Visible Ink Press, 1996. p. 684.

Heptathlon Activities and Discussion Questions

1. Read about the ancient Olympic Games and note some of the events the Greeks included for throwing, jumping, and running. Write a brief newspaper article describing one of the ancient events in detail. Add a catchy headline to the article and an illustration. Remember to include who, what, where, when, why and how. Also, include the distances for the foot races and the materials they used for the other events. Try adding interviews with the athletes and have some fun going back in time to 776 B.C.!

2. The six women athletes in the list below have been compared to each other and each has been given the title "Greatest Woman Athlete" in books or articles.

   Choose the name of one woman out of six from a hat and research her accomplishments. Then, consider some of the factors listed below to determine why the woman you researched is the "greatest" athlete. Write a brief persuasive speech and present it to your class on why "The Greatest Athlete of the Year" Award should be given to _____.

   Have the class take a vote after all the speeches have been given.

   "Greatest Woman Athlete" Candidates

Irena Szewinska (Poland)	Fanny Blankers-Koen (Holland)
Wilma Rudolph (U.S.)	Babe Didrikson (U.S.)
Florence Griffith-Joyner (U.S.)	Jackie Joyner-Kersee (U.S.)

   Winning Characteristics

Fastest Runner	Most Versatile in Many Events
Has Received the Most Medals	Greatest Endurance
Has Won Many Competitions	Has Competed in the Olympics the Most Years

3. Write to the President's Council on Physical Fitness and Sports (701 Pennsylvania Avenue, N.W. Suite 250, Washington, DC. 20004) to find out what type of fitness standards are set for boys and girls between the ages six and seventeen. Why does The President's Council measure fitness in terms of curl-ups, pull-ups, a shuttle run, one-mile run, and the sit and reach (V-Sit).

Learning Objectives: To introduce students to the Ancient Game events. To think of the versatility and training an athlete must have to compete in a heptathlon or several events. To consider qualities of the "greatest athlete" title. To discover what fitness tests are and compare fitness levels with the national average.

Swimming

Competitive swimming began in England in the 1830s. At that time the breast stroke was the most common method of swimming. While travelling to Australia from England, Fredrick Cavill noticed the powerful stroke used by inhabitants of the South Sea Islands. Cavill learned this new method of swimming and taught it to swimmers in Australia, England and the United States. The new stroke eventually transformed the sport.

During the 1896 Olympic Games, competitors swam on the coast of Greece in the Bay of Zea. The temperature of the water was 55° Fahrenheit (F), (13° Centigrade (C)). In the Paris Games in 1900, the swimmers competed in the Seine River. The 1904 Games in St. Louis offered a pool situated in the middle of a man-made lake. Seating arrangements for spectators were problematic. After the 1904 Games, a 50-meter pool with eight lanes became the standard for Olympic events. The temperature of the water ranged from 70–80° F (25.5–26.6° C).

Strategy

To achieve faster times, swimmers must pay attention to efficient stroke movements, quick starts, and clean turns. Like a running race, a swimming event begins with a starting gun or an electronic tone. A false start disqualifies the swimmer. Depending on the distance of the race, the swimmer concentrates on all out speed in short races or consistent pacing in longer ones. Some may opt to swim a "negative split" which means swimming the first half of a race slower than the second half.

Styles of Swimming Strokes

Freestyle As the name implies, swimmers are free to choose the stroke. In most cases, the Australian crawl is used with the arms following an overhand motion.

Butterfly One of the most difficult strokes to learn and coordinate, it combines overhand motions of the arms with a dolphin kick. It became popular in the 1950s.

Backstroke The swimmer lies on her back and propels herself through the water with alternating overhead arm motions and a flutter kick.

Breaststroke The breaststroke requires the swimmer to simultaneously move her arms and legs while using a frog kick.

In an individual medley race one swimmer will swim all four strokes. A medley relay race will include four different swimmers each swimming a different style of stroke.

Famous Swimmers in Olympic History

<u>Johnny Weissmuller</u> United States; Paris, 1924, Amsterdam, 1928.
Johnny Weissmuller won five gold medals between 1924 and 1928. Two years before the Paris Games he swam the 100-meter race in less than one minute. No one had

done that before. In Paris, he won a gold in the 100-meter freestyle, 400-meter freestyle and the 4x200-meter freestyle relay. During the 100-meter freestyle race in 1928, Weissmuller swallowed some water and nearly lost consciousness. He recovered within seconds, took the lead and won the race by about a second. Four years later, Weismuller was modeling swimsuits for the BVD Underwear Company. A Hollywood film executive saw photos of Weismuller in a swimsuit, and this connection led him into an acting career as Tarzan. *Tarzan, the Ape Man*, his first film, debuted in 1932. He eventually made twelve films.

Dawn Fraser Australia; Melbourne, 1956; Rome, 1960 ;Tokyo, 1964.
Known for her tremendous speed, determination, rebellious spirit, and antics, Fraser became the first Olympic swimmer to capture a gold for the same event in three consecutive summer Olympics. No other man or woman has achieved this honor. At nineteen, Frazer competed in her first international competition in Melbourne. In her autobiography, *Below the Surface* she writes about a nightmare she had the night before the race. First, she dreamed that honey on the starting block held her feet so tightly that she could not dive in the pool. Then as she dove into the pool, the water turned into spaghetti. Regardless of her nervousness, on the following day she won the 100-meters by 3/10 of a second and broke the world record. Four years later she captured the gold again.

Mark Spitz United States, Mexico City, 1968 ; Munich, 1972.
Spitz holds the record for winning the most medals in one Olympic year. He won four in individual events and three in relay events. Spitz broke world records in the 100-meter and 200-meter freestyle, the 100 and 200-meter butterfly, the 4x100-meter freestyle relay, the 4x100-medley relay, and the 4x200-meter freestyle. Spitz signed numerous contracts for commercial endorsements following the Munich Olympics. In the first year after the 1972 Games he earned close to five million dollars in endorsements.

Kristin Otto German; Seoul, 1988.
In the 1988 Olympics Otto won a gold medal in each of six events: 50-meter freestyle, 100-meter freestyle, 100-meter backstroke, 100-meter butterfly, 4x100-meter freestyle relay and 4x100-meter medley relay. Her versatility in winning three different styles of swimming (freestyle, backstroke, butterfly) is unsurpassed in history. She holds the record for the most gold medals won by a woman in any single Olympic year.

Further Reading

Counsilman, James E. *The New Science of Swimming*. Englewood Cliffs, NJ: Prentice Hall, 1994. 420 pp. Technical manual describing the latest theories and scientific findings on the mechanics of swimming strokes. Reading level: 8th grade–Adult.

Duder, Tessa. *In Lane Three, Alex Archer*. New York: Houghton Mifflin Co., 1987. 175 pp. A story about a fifteen-year-old meeting her toughest competitor in the 1980 Olympics. Fiction. Reading level: 6th–10th grade. (Also *Alex in Rome*, 1991)

American Red Cross. *Swimming and Diving*. St. Louis, MO: Mosby Lifeline, 1992. 354 pp. Superbly instructive with updated information on swimming techniques, this is an outstanding resource for a comprehensive look at swimming and diving.

Swimming Activities and Discussion Questions

1. Similes:Finish the sentences below with a phrase that creates an image.
   A swimming pool is like….
   Lane markers look like….
   When she does a flip turn she looks like….
   The diving board looks like….
   Goggles on a swimmer look like….
   A long shallow dive looks like….
   A buoy is like a ….
   A swimmer doing the backstroke looks like….

2. Research the three types of body shape: endomorphy, mesomorphy, and ectomorphy. Create a visual chart or display to link each body shape with the sports that generally match it. You may want to work in three different groups and have three different types of presentation. What body type are you? Do you think people are restricted only to the activities that generally match their body type? Why or why not?

3. Performance Comparisons: Since swimmers improve their mechanics of strokes and strive to improve their times each year, Olympic champions from years ago could not compete at the same top levels in the world today. For example, Mark Spitz won seven gold medals in 1972, but his record times then would not place him in the top 25 Olympic swimmers today. Johnny Weissmuller won the 100m race in 1928. His winning time would not have been in the qualifying times for the women swimming in the finals in 1976. Use the information below to discuss the drastic changes in times and make comparisons to other events, if you wish. Make your own chart including more times and the event of your choice.

Women 100m		**Freestyle Men**	
1912	1:22.2	1912	1:03.40
1980	54.79	1980	50.40
1992	54.64	1992	49.02

Learning Objectives: To create similes from sentences related to swimming. To compare body types of swimmers to other sports. To chart swimming records from 1912 and compare them to 1980 and 1992 times.

Fencing

Fencing, like fist fighting, has been part of human history for thousands of years as a method of combat. The first record of the sport of fencing dates back to 1190 B.C. in Egypt. A relief depicting two sword fighters wearing protective gear, umpires, spectators, and organizers dates back to this time period.

The French, Germans, and Italians influenced many of the rules and standards for modern fencing. Many believed the practice of fencing was an art similar to chess, involving strategy, attacking moves, counter-moves, and patience. In the 1700s G. Danet and D. Angelo wrote several articles on fencing and established many of the rules and approaches to scoring.

Fencing was included as one of the sports in the first Olympics. The Baron Pierre de Coubertin, founder of the modern Olympics, was a fencer, and that might have contributed to the decision to include fencing among the events. In many of the Olympics, participants from the European countries of France, Italy, Spain, Great Britain, the former Soviet Union, and the Netherlands have dominated the sport.

Strategy

Fencing requires concentration, efficient movement, timing, anticipation, and an element of surprise. The object is to score points by touching the opponent in the scoring area. Because judges may not follow the foils as quickly as they move, electronic devices keep track of the touches between opponents. However, judges tally their own points by observing the distance midway between the two fencers.

Equipment

Foil It is three feet long (30 cm) and weighs 17⅝ oz. (500 g). The blade is four-sided and the shape of the handle varies according to the preferences of the fencer. The target area for the foil is the torso.

Epee Similar in length to the foil, the epee weighs up to 27.16 ounces (770 g). The blade is shaped like a triangle on a cross-section. The target area for the epee is the entire body, as the sword evolved from those used in duels meant only to draw blood, not kill.

Sabre The sabre's length is 41.338 inches (1050 millimeters) and it weighs the same as the foil. Points may be scored with slicing or cutting motions in addition to thrusting moves. The target area for sabre fencing is the head and torso above the waist, since the weapon evolved from the cavalry sabre used by mounted soldiers.

Famous Fencers in Olympic History

<u>Nedo Nadi</u> Italy; Stockholm, 1912; Antwerp, 1920.
Nadi competed in 1912, when he was eighteen years old. He won the gold, and another Italian, Pietro Speciale, won the silver. Four years later, Nadi repeated his

Fencing Bouts
Once begun, bouts continue until one fencer makes five touches (four for women) or six minutes have passed.

victory in the individual foil competition, and added four other gold medals in the individual sabre, and the team events for the foil, sabre, and epee.

Adolfo Contronei Italy; Paris, 1924.
During the team foil competition, the French and Italians were in the finals for the gold medal. Lucien Gaudin and Aldo Boni were tied when the jury gave Gaudin a fifth touch. Boni was infuriated by the decision and he verbally abused the Hungarian judge, who was named Kovacs. Kovacs demanded an apology from Boni in front of the Jury of Appeal. Boni refused, saying he had not done anything. Kovacs called in Italo Santelli, an Italian of Hungarian descent to back up his charges. Santelli agreed with Kovacs. The Italian team withdrew from competition altogether, but the differences of opinion were not settled. After returning home, the Italian team wrote a statement to Santelli accusing him of meddling in the French and Italian final to ensure a victory for the Hungarian fencing team. Santelli became so irate that he challenged the captain of the Italian team, Adolfo Contronei, to a duel. After Santelli's son, Giorgio, heard about the duel, he asked to fight in his father's place. Italo was 60 years old and his son was 27. The duel took place in Ahazzia. Using heavy sabres, Santelli and Contronei fought for two minutes until Santelli grazed Contronei on the side of the head. The duel ended. Giorgio continued his fencing, eventually moving to the United States to teach the U.S. team.

Helene Mayer Germany; Amsterdam, 1928; Los Angeles, 1932; Berlin, 1936.
Mayer was a German Jew who won her first gold medal in 1928 in the individual foil. Four years later she finished in fifth place. That same year, she moved to the United States to teach German at Mills College. When the Germans hosted the 1936 Olympics in Berlin, they formally invited her to compete for Germany, even though they made it clear that Jews were not generally welcome. Even though Mayer's father was Jewish, the Germans extended their permission because her grandparents were "Aryan." Going into the final round in the Berlin Olympics, Mayer was tied with Ilona Schacherer-Elek, a Hungarian Jew. The first encounter score was 2–2. The second match was 3–3. The third score was 4–4. It was still a draw and the judges decided to choose a winner based on points. Schacherer-Elek won the gold, Mayer won the silver. On the platform receiving the medals, Helene Mayer saluted Hitler and the audience applauded in response.

Further Reading

Greenspan, Bud. *100 Greatest Moments in Olympic History*. Los Angeles, CA: General Publishing Group, Inc., 1995. 224 pp. This contains a brief story about George S. Patton, who fenced in the pentathlon, as well as other Olympic champions. Reading level: 4th grade–Adult.

Johnson, William Oscar. *The Olympics: A History of the Games*. Birmingham, AL: Oxmoor House, 1992. 224 pp. This oversized book covers the spectacular moments and personalities in Olympic history. Extraordinary color and black and white photos included. Reading level: 8th grade–Adult.

Nelson, Rebecca and Marie J. MacNee. *The Olympic Factbook*. Detroit, MI: Visible Ink Press, 1996. 855 pp. Comprehensive guide on the events and hopefuls in each event. Detailed description of the rules and equipment for fencing. Reading level: 5th grade–Adult.

Protective equipment for the fencer includes: a mask with wire mesh, gloves, a padded vest, and a padded jacket.

Fencing Activities and Discussion Questions

1. Fencing Scenes in Movies: Dramatic presentations of conflicts in movies may involve a fencing bout, depending on the time period of the movie. In *The Princess Bride* and *The Three Musketeers* swordfighting separates the hero from the villain. In a futuristic movie like *Star Wars* the characters use light sabers for weapons. Why do you think the director for this movie wanted to include a fencing-type weapon, instead of using a phaser or a gun? As a class, list all the movies you can think of with fencing bouts in the story. Are all the films part of the same time period?

2. What are the most popular combat sports portrayed in books, movies and television today? Rank the following, with a score of one for the most popular and ten for the least popular.

   Judo   Fencing   Boxing
   Karate   Wrestling   Kendo

3. Write a short story using the characters and events below as a basis.

   - One of the characters in your story is an expert fencing champion.
   - Set the clock back to the 1300s or anytime before that for the time period of your story.
   - At the beginning of the story, someone has stolen your horse.

   Now you may finish the rest.

Learning Objectives: To study the image of fencing in movies. To relate it to modern day combat sports. To learn about writing short stories.

Boxing

Though fist fighting existed much earlier than the ancient Olympic games, the first time boxing became part of the Olympics was in 688 B.C. At that time, boxers wore leather thongs around their fists and they fought until one man fell down or raised his hand in surrender.

The Romans witnessed fights ending in death or near death when boxers were allowed to wear gloves with spikes, nails or metal balls. Excavated busts of the athletes participating in these boxing matches showed missing ears or noses due to the brutal blows to the head. When the Roman Empire fell, people lost interest in boxing. But in the 1600s, an Englishman named James Figg introduced a new form that combined bare knuckles and fencing strategies. As the sport evolved, the amount of brutality decreased. In the 1800s the Marquis of Queensberry introduced rules that are still part of the sport.

In Athens, boxing was excluded as an event due to its history of brutality. By 1904 its popularity had spread, and it became an Olympic event. Women also participated in boxing in 1904. In 1912 boxing was banned from the Olympics because it was against the law to box in Sweden, however it was restored as an event in subsequent Olympics.

Boxing Rules

Each match consists of three rounds lasting three minutes. Winners advance to the next level in one of twelve weight classes.

Olympic Boxing Rules

Each boxer will participate in three rounds lasting three minutes. Between each round is a one-minute rest period. If the boxer falls on the canvas or hangs onto the outside ropes, he is considered down.

The objective is to score the highest number of points awarded by the judges or knock out the opponent. Five judges (usually from five different continents) award the points using computers. Judges watch the white part of the boxing gloves to determine blows. The winners of each match advance to the next level. There are twelve weight classes in Olympic boxing.

Judges often watch the midpoint between the two boxers to determine which one is throwing more punches. The third round becomes an endurance test for both competitors.

Strategy

Modern boxers use quick movements and jabs to work an opponent much like fencing. Most Olympic boxers prefer to score points rather than to win by a knockout. Some use a "stick-and-move" technique, meaning they throw a punch and dart quickly out of reach.

Famous Boxers in Olympic History

Muhammad Ali (Cassius Clay) United States; Rome, 1960.
When he was only eighteen years old, Cassius Clay won an Olympic gold medal in the light heavyweight (179 lbs.–81 kg.) class. Proud of his achievement, he wore the

medal on many occasions. Unfortunately, neither the medal nor the achievement could break down the walls between whites and African Americans. One day he visited a white restaurant wearing his gold medal, but the waitress refused to serve him. When he insisted on his right to service, she called the manager, who forced Clay to leave. Clay and a friend left the restaurant, but a group of white men followed them and asked for the gold medal. Clay refused to give it to them. He fled and the men chased him on motorcycles. They started a fight, close to the Ohio river. Clay and his friend Ronnie King won. While cleaning their bleeding hands in the river, Clay realized how ordinary the gold medal really was. He threw it in the river. Clay became a professional boxer in the heavyweight class. He held titles in 1964–70, 1974–78, 1978–79. He changed his name to Muhammad Ali after he won the title in 1964.

Teofilo Stevenson Cuba; Munich, 1972; Montreal, 1976; Moscow, 1980.
Fighting in the heavyweight division (200 lbs. - 91 kg.), Stevenson captured the gold in Munich without much difficulty. He beat Peter Hussing in the semifinals in only four minutes and three seconds. After winning the gold, many promoters wanted Stevenson to become a professional boxer. He turned down a $2 million offer observing that professional boxing treats a fighter like a commodity to be bought and sold and discarded when he is no longer of use. Stevenson opted to continue his education. In 1976, he won another gold medal, which he repeated in 1980, becoming the first to win three consecutive gold medals in the heavyweight class.

László Papp Hungary; London, 1948; Helsinki, 1952; Melbourne, 1956.
Papp fought in the middleweight division and won the gold medal in 1948. The next year he choose the light-middleweight division, again winning easily with two knockouts. He captured a third gold in Melbourne in a bout against Jose Torres from the United States. Papp became the first boxer to win three gold medals. After becoming a professional boxer, he fought 30 times without one defeat.

Oscar De La Hoya United States; Barcelona, 1992.
Nicknamed the Golden Boy by the Mexican American community, De La Hoya won the gold medal in the lightweight division in 1992. He had promised his mother, who died of cancer in 1990, that he would win a gold medal, so he dedicated the medal to her. Although he has become a professional boxer and has earned over a million dollars, De La Hoya still remembers his mother and his roots. He keeps a $1 food stamp in his wallet to remind him of the days when his mother would send him to the grocery store with food stamps.

Further Reading

Conklin, Thomas. *Muhammad Ali*. Brookfield, CT: Millbrook Press, 1992. 101 pp. Presents the controversies and fights Muhammad Ali fought outside and inside the ring. Reading level: 5th–10th grade.

Fleischer, Nat and Sam E. Andre. *A Pictorial History of Boxing*. New York: Carol Publishing Group, 1993. Comprehensive historical guide to boxing including hundreds of pictures. Reading level: 4th grade–Adult.

Suster, Gerald. *Champions of the Ring*. Great Britain: Robson Books. 1992. 326 pp. Covers the boxing careers of all the world heavyweight champions. Reading level: 8th grade–Adult.

Boxing Activities and Discussion Questions

1. Using at least fifteen prepositions (under, between, into, above, through, etc.) write a short article about a boxing match. Pretend you are in the stands watching and describing the moves, jabs, and footwork. Be imaginative!

2. In 1990, when Muhammad Ali was asked to participate in the documentary *Eyes on the Prize* he responded, "Why do they want me to be in this film? What did I do to be with all those great people?" Do you believe Muhammad Ali was one of the greatest boxers of all time? Read together the chapter in Bill Littlefield's *Champions* and discuss whether you think Ali was truly great.

3. Using reference books from your school or local library, write a brief personal profile in your own words about one of the following heavyweight champions.

   Jack Dempsey   Joe Louis
   Rocky Marciano   Joe Frazier
   George Foreman   Leon Spinks
   Larry Holmes

4. Radio Boxing Match: Before television and movies, children and adults gathered around the radio for evening entertainment. Even boxing matches came to life in the living rooms. Stage an imaginary boxing match and have one or two students take turns being broadcasters. If you have time, give your radio sports program the ultimate test. Record it and play it back to a small group of students. Does the language you use create suspense for the listeners? Can you describe the action with such detail that even those who are not watching can experience it? Challenge yourself with this project. If you need help, study the professionals. Listen to National Public Radio and be attentive to the way they draw images over the air waves.

Learning Objectives: To write an imaginative short piece about a boxing match. To focus on one well-known personality in boxing history. To use rich images and language to create a radio program about a suspenseful boxing match.

Shooting

The invention of firearms in the 1300s led to shooting competitions. Baron Pierre de Coubertin, the founder of the modern Olympics, included shooting in the 1896 Games because he was a fine marksman and enjoyed the sport as a boy.

Olympic shooting has expanded from five events in 1896 to thirteen events in 1996. Pistols, rifles, and shotguns are used in the variety of events depending on the type of target and range. Many of the competitors have had military or other special training. The age or size of the competitor has very little to do with the ability of the marksman. In some events, men and women compete against each other. What is common to most participants, however, is a steady hand, a keen eye, patience, and endurance (some competitors shoot for two hours at a time). The shooters who advance to the final round are contenders for a medal. In the pistol and rifle events, it is the top eight, in the running target and shotgun events, the top six finishers may win a medal.

Competition is offered in the following categories:
Rapid-fire Pistol

Standing twenty-five meters away from the target, the competitor gives a "ready" signal and five targets are presented. The shooter fires 30 times at a 4" bull's-eye with a .22 caliber pistol. The goal is to place five shots in the bull's-eye within eight seconds, then five shots within six seconds, and five within four seconds. The event is for men only.

Running Game Target

Using a .177 caliber air rifle with telescopic sights, a shooter stands ten meters from a target of a boar-shaped animal. The bull's-eye is 15.5 millimeters. The participant is allowed 30 shots when the target is moving slowly and another 30 shots when it is moving twice as fast. Again, the event is for men only.

Trap Shooting

Using a 12-gauge shotgun, the shooter calls "pull" and a clay target flies upward from a trap pit fifteen meters from the marksman. At times the clay target may travel at up to 100 mph. The shooters have only one and a half seconds to hit the target. They are allowed 25 shots in a total of eight rounds. The competition is for both men and women, and extends for three days.

Skeet Shooting

Similar to trap shooting, the marksmen and women use 12-gauge shotguns, but they must hold the gun at their waist. Targets are sent into the air from two bases without any warning or signals. They shoot a total of 200 times in groups of 25. This competition also extends over three days.

Famous Shooters in Olympic History

Károly Takács Hungary; London, 1948; Helsinki, 1952.
In 1938 Takács was one of the world's most accurate pistol shooters. He served in the Hungarian Army as a sergeant. One day while he was practicing drills, a hand grenade exploded in his right hand, completely destroying it. During the month Takács spent in the hospital, he decided to learn how to shoot a pistol left-handed. Secretly, he practiced on his own. When he attended a pistol shooting competition in 1939, most of his friends thought he came to watch. They were surprised when they learned that he was planning to compete. To their greater surprise, Takács won the competition. In 1948 Takács qualified for Hungary's Olympic shooting team, and subsequently won a gold medal. At that time he was 38-years old. In 1952 he captured the gold again by a margin of one point over another Hungarian, Szalard Kun.

Margaret Murdock United States; Montreal, 1976.
Murdock won the silver in the three-position shooting competition, shooting against male competitors, to become the first woman to win in an Olympic shooting event.

Oscar Swahn Sweden; London, 1908, 1912, 1920 & 1924.
Swahn went on record as one of the oldest competitors in the Olympic Games. He won a gold in running deer shooting when he was 60 years old. In 1912 he won a gold and a bronze; in 1920 he won a silver. Twelve years later, at age 72, he won another medal and in 1924 he medaled again.

Zhang Shan China; Barcelona, 1992.
Shan became famous when she won the skeet shooting competition in Barcelona in which both men and women participated. Shan scored 223 points out of a possible 225 to break the Olympic record. She is the first woman to win a gold medal in a shooting competition open to both men and women competitors. Since the games in Barcelona, the International Shooting Union changed the rules for the Olympics so men and women will compete separately in shooting events.

Antonius Limberkovitz Hungary; Los Angeles, 1932.
In the prone rifle event, Limberkovitz fired and hit the bull's-eye of a target next to his own. He told the officials he hit the wrong target. If he hadn't reported the error, he would have won the gold medal. The officials declared his shot a miss; and he lost the chance for a medal.

Further Reading

Young, Mark. *The Guinness Book of Sports Records 1994-1995*. New York: Facts on File, 1994. 250 pp. Provides information and updated records on over 30 different sports, including pistol shooting. Reading level: 4th grade–Adult.

Greenspan, Bud. *100 Greatest Moments in Olympic History*. Los Angeles: General Publishing Group, 1995. 224 pp. Covers the accomplishments of great Olympic athletes in modern history, including Karoly Takacs. Reading level: 4th-Adult.

Diagram Group. *The Sports Fan's Ultimate Book of Sports Comparisons*. New York: St. Martin's Press, 1982. 192 pp. In the section on target sports, this book compares the projectiles used for shooting, the weapons used, and the speed of the bullets. Reading level: 3rd grade–Adult.

Shooting Activities and Discussion Questions

1. Use a sports record book or almanac to complete these sentences.

    In 1967 _____ participated in the smallbore rifle competition against men and won the competition.

    Carl Osburn (United States) won _____medals in Olympic competition. He holds a record for the most medals.

    In 1992, Marina Logvinenko (Unified Team) captured two medals in _____and _____.

    In 1988, Ragnar Skanaker was _____years old when he won the silver medal.

2. Classify the pistols and rifles into groups according to size and distances of the targets.

3. In target sports like pistol shooting, superb concentration and sharp precision are essential to the athletes' performance. Some target shooters go into a Zen-type state of mind. What is Zen? How could a Zen state of mind be beneficial to pistol shooters?

Learning Objectives: To learn new facts about pistol shooting. To study the equipment used in pistol shooting. To explore the benefits of Zen concentration.

Answers to question 1: 1. Margaret Murdock, 2. 11, 3. sport pistol and air pistol, 4. 54.

Equestrian

Horses were introduced into Olympic competition in the ancient games of 688 B.C. for chariot racing, and horseback riding events in 648 B.C. The development of modern equestrian events took place in Naples and Vienna in the 1500s with schools offering classical training. Show jumping became popular in the early part of the nineteenth century when only one fence stood as the obstacle. It was included for the first time in the modern Olympics in 1912, together with dressage and the three-day equestrian event. Women competed in show jumping for the first time during the Stockholm Games in 1956.

Military training and equestrian events have evolved together over the years. The three-day event follows the guidelines set for training horses in the cavalry or military. Horses must exhibit obedience and elegance in dressage; they must have endurance and courage to run long distances for the cross-country race; and demonstrate jumping abilities in the show jumping competition.

Dressage
Show Jumping
Three-day event

Tests of obedience, elegance, endurance and courage are intermixed in three major categories.

Equestrian Events

Dressage This is an indoor event. To perform the riders must wear a formal jacket, gloves, top hat or riding hat, and boots. Each rider must guide his or her horse through a series of maneuvers to demonstrate superb training and obedience. Judges award points between 0 and 10 for the presentation. The following are examples of maneuvers:

> Flying change: skipping
> Piaffe: horse lifts his knees to the left and right while standing in one place
> Reinback: walking backwards
> Side Pass: walking the horse forward and to one side at the same time

Dressage is a French word, meaning "to train." The origin of this event dates back to Medieval times, though the Renaissance furthered its development.

Show Jumping The course ranges from 700 to 900 meters long with up to fifteen obstacles for the horse and rider to jump. Instead of using obstacles of uniform size, there are vertical jumps of different heights, water jumps, a stone wall obstacle and spreads with double or triple planes set up horizontally. If a horse refuses to jump over an obstacle, that is equal to three faults. A knockdown is worth four faults. Riders try to score the least number of faults possible.

Three-Day Event Besides show jumping and dressage, the cross-county events test the stamina and confidence of the rider and horse over a long distance race of twenty-one kilometers. Along the roads and trails are obstacles such as log jumps, ramps or water jumps. In addition the course includes a steeplechase with eight to ten barriers. Horses do not have a chance to practice on the course before the Olympic competition, though the riders receive a map of the course to anticipate the obstacles.

Famous Equestrian Competitors in Olympic History

Henri Saint Cyr Sweden; London, 1948; Helsinki, 1952; Stockholm, 1956.
Cyr won four gold medals: two in the dressage individual and team event in 1952, and two in the same events in Stockholm four years later.

Lis Hartel Denmark; Helsinki, 1952; Stockholm, 1956.
Women were not allowed to enter equestrian events before the Helsinki Games in 1952, but that year four women competed. One of these four women, Lis Hartel, participated despite the fact that in 1944 she had acquired polio which paralyzed her legs. Before this illness she was one of the best riders in Denmark. Gradually, she developed the thigh muscles necessary to ride again. Below the knees she remained paralyzed. She won the silver medal in 1952, though she could not mount or dismount her horse by herself. When it came time for the awards ceremony the gold medalist, Henri Saint Cyr, helped her onto the platform to receive her silver medal.

Kathy Kusner United States; Mexico City, 1968; Munich, 1972.
Kusner participated in the team show jumping competition. She placed fourth in Mexico City and won the silver in the same event in 1972. One of Kusner's dreams as a girl was to become a jockey, but up to that time women were not allowed in racing events as jockeys. Once the Civil Rights Act (1964) changed the laws forbidding discrimination against women, Kusner believed she could fight for her rights through the legal system. In 1968 Kathy Kusner became the first licensed female jockey in the United States. One year later on the Pocono Downs track in Pennsylvania she won her first race.

Karen Stives United States; Los Angeles, 1984.
Coming into the final round, Stives was in first place. However, she needed to clear twelve obstacles before winning the gold medal. On the eleventh obstacle her horse nicked the top of the fence, causing five faults. She finished in second place in the individual three-day event, but won the gold in the team event with her teammates Torrance Watkins Fleischmann and J. Michael Plumb.

Further Reading

Callahan, Dorothy. *Julie Krone*. Minneapolis, MN: Dillon Press, 1990. 64 pp. This book focuses on the life and achievements of one of the greatest female jockeys in the world. Reading level: 3rd–6th grade.

Green, Lucinda. *The Young Rider*. New York, NY: Dorling Kindersley, 1993. 64 pp. This photo-filled, instructive guide is highly recommended for school libraries. It covers every aspect of riding including choosing a riding school, grooming a horse, and showing horses. Reading level: 3rd–8th grade.

Woolum, Janet. *Outstanding Women Athletes*. Phoenix, AZ: The Oryx Press. 1992. 279 pp. An informative and inspiring resource on hundreds of women athletes who competed in Olympic events and professional sports throughout history. Highly recommended for elementary and middle school libraries. Reading level: 5th–12th grade.

Equestrian Activities and Discussion Questions

1. Equestrian Equipment: Contact a local 4H group or stables in your community to invite a horseback rider or instructor to show some of the gear used for the equestrian dressage event. As a class, write out ten questions about equipment for the horses, maintenance, and what species of horses are best suited for each Olympic event.

2. Should men and women compete together? When Kathy Kusner tried to convince men that she would be capable of becoming a jockey, she pointed out that horseback riding required skill and technique more than brute strength. She compared equestrian competitions to chess games where it doesn't matter if women competed against men. Rank the following sports and games in terms of whether they should separate women competitors from men or not. One point means it should be separate, and ten points means it should not be separate.

   ____ Skiing   ____ Table Tennis   ____ Swimming
   ____ Golf   ____ Archery   ____ Cycling
   ____ Bowling   ____ Tennis   ____ Diving
   ____ Chess   ____ Auto Racing   ____ Dog Sled Racing
   ____ Pistol Shooting   ____ Street Hockey ____ Gymnastics
   ____ Rock Climbing   ____ Marathon Running
   ____ Equestrian Events

3. Sites of Past Olympic Games: Using a photocopy of pages from an atlas or a large world map, place a tack or pin in each of the sites of past Olympic Games. In small groups, write a brief persuasive speech arguing for a site of your choice for the Olympics in the year 2000. Think of an ideal setting anywhere in the world. You may have to research some of these sites to know how they were chosen.

Learning Objectives: To learn about horses and the gear for showing at a stable. To discuss sports men and women may participate in equally. To use the power of persuasion to select a site for a Summer Olympic Games.

Yachting

Early sailboats or "jaghtschips," as the Dutch called them were used in the 1600s to guard cargo ships from pirates during their ocean journeys. "Jaght" meant to hunt or chase, and the Dutch specialized in designing and building these fast and maneuverable boats.

King Charles II introduced the sailboat to the British, though he changed its name to yacht. The first sailing club (Water Club of the Harbour of Cork) was founded in Ireland in 1720. The sport of yachting became popular in the United States approximately one hundred years later.

Yachting was among the events in the first modern Olympics in 1896, but poor weather caused the officials to cancel the races. One of the difficulties that arose during Olympic competition was developing a rating system for the various sizes of sailboats, since there was no uniformity in length and weight. Following the adoption of the International Rule of 1906, the International Yacht Racing Union developed a standard rating system for sailboats which placed limits on their design.

Classes of Yachts

Since 1920, the following sailboat classes have been recognized for Olympic competition:

Finn A 14' 9", one person, centerboard dinghy. (men only)

Europe An 11', one person, centerboard dinghy. (women only)

470 A 15' 5", two person, dinghy. (men and women separate)

Laser A 13' 11", one person, dinghy. (men and women separate)

Mistral IMCO A 12' 2" sailboard. (men and women separate)

Soling A 26' 11", three person keelboat.

Star A 22' 8", two person keelboat.

Tornado A 20', two person catamaran.

The Event

Yachts begin at a marker (indicated by buoys) and must round the buoys in a particular order along the course to the finish line. The distance of the course may vary according to the class of the yacht, but the average distance is eleven miles. One of the most dramatic phases to watch is the start of the race. Warning signals are given at set intervals to prepare the racers. If a yacht crosses the starting line before the starting gun or horn sounds, that yacht is disqualified. Yachts with the lowest scores are the winners.

Technique

Going upwind, the sailor uses a technique called "tacking" which involves sailing 45 degrees at an angle into the wind. The path of this course is Z-shaped. Going downwind, the wind may push the boat directly toward its target and this is called "running with the wind." Superb sailors check constantly for shifts in the wind to give them an advantage over their opponents.

Famous Sailors in Olympic History

Paul Elvstrom Denmark; London, 1948; Helsinki, 1952; Melbourne, 1956; Rome-Naples, 1960; Munich, 1972.
Elvstrom won the gold medal in the Finn yachting class in 1948, 1952, 1956, and 1960. In 1972, he attempted to become the first person to win five gold medals in five different Games. While he raced in the Soling class, another boat bumped into him; and this angered him so much he left the Olympics before finishing all his races.

Durward Knowles Bahamas; London, 1948; Helsinki, 1952; Melbourne, 1956; Rome-Naples, 1960; Tokyo, 1964.
Knowles competed in five Olympic Games racing in the Star class. He placed fourth in 1948, fifth in 1952, third in 1956, sixth in 1960, and won the gold medal in 1964 by a margin of only six seconds!

Magnus Konow Norway; London-Ryde, 1908; Antwerp, 1920; Amsterdam, 1928; London, 1948.
Magnus Konow competed in the eight-meter class in 1908 and forty years later competed in the six-meter class. He won the gold in 1920 with his teammates Reidar Marthiniussen, Ragnar Vig, and Thorleif Christoffersen.

Royal Sailors in Olympic History

Crown Prince Ola Norway; Amsterdam, 1928.
Soon to become King Olav V, the Crown Prince won the gold medal with three other sailors in the six-meter class.

Crown Prince Constantin Greece; Rome-Naples, 1960.
After winning the gold medal in the Dragon class with two other sailors, Constantin's mother, Queen Frederika, pushed him into the water as a victory celebration.

Queen Sofia Spain; Rome-Naples, 1960.

King Juan Carlo Spain; Munich, 1972.
King Carlos participated in the 1972 Games; his daughter competed in 1988 and his son raced in the Soling class in 1992.

Further Reading

Blake, Peter and David Pardon. *An Introduction to Sailing*. Dobbs Ferry, NY: Sheridan House, 1993. 128 pp. The author, a sailor from New Zealand, presents a practical guide on learning to sail. Photos and diagrams included. Reading level: 6th grade–Adult.

Phillips-Birt, Douglas. *The History of Yachting*. New York: Stein and Day, 1974. 288 pp. Comprehensive coverage of yachting as a sport. Photos and drawing included in this oversized book. Reading level: 6th grade–Adult.

Vandervoort, Thomas J. *Sailing Is for Me*. Minneapolis, MN: Lerner Publications. 1981. 48 pp. Excellent guide for teaching students about the designs of sailboats and the terms used for sailing. Follows an eleven-year-old boy and his sister through the process of sailing a dinghy. Reading level: 4th-6th grade.

Yachting Activities and Discussion Questions

1. Know Your Yachting Terms Before You Sail: Look up the following terms in a dictionary or a yachting glossary, then in groups of three or four, write a story using the vocabulary word in each sentence. Take turns adding the sentences.

ballast	hike or hike out
beating	jib
boom	keel
centerboard	leg
heeling	mast
rudder	run
tacking	trapeze

2. America's Cup: One of the most prestigious races in yachting, read about the America's Cup and answer the following questions about this race.
   In what year was the first America's Cup race?
   Who won the first race?
   How long was the actual race?
   Which country has dominated this race for many years?

3. Classify the yachts used in the Olympics according to size. Be sure to mark down the dimensions of the boat and the sail. Research the potential speed each boat may travel.

4. Read *The Dove* by Robin Graham and discuss it as a class.

Learning Objectives: To learn terms related to yachting. To research one of the oldest yachting races, the America's Cup. To classify the yachts used in the Olympics. To read a novel about sailing around the world.

Answers to question 2: The first race was held in 1851 in Great Britain; America; 58 miles; The United States.

Basketball

Twelve teams will compete in both men's and women's basketball.

Dr. James A. Naismith invented basketball as a method to keep athletes in condition during winter months in 1891. Naismith was a physical education teacher at the International YMCA Training College in Springfield, Massachusetts, known today as Springfield College. Naismith's original notion about basketball excluded any physical contact. For hoops, he simply nailed two peach baskets to the balcony, ten feet above the gymnasium floor. Basketballs had not been invented, so the first students who tested the sport played with a soccer ball. Naismith developed only thirteen rules for basketball at that time. Even though the game evolved into a more sophisticated and precise sport, many of the rules Naismith devised are part of basketball today.

In 1936 basketball became an Olympic sport, though it had been a demonstration sport in 1904, 1924, and 1928. At that time the game was played outdoors on a clay tennis court. The U.S. actually sent two basketball teams in 1936; one team named the McPherson Globe Oilers played in the finals against Canada. During the course of the final game, a rainstorm hit and flooded the clay court. As a result, only eight points were scored in the second half of the game, four for each team! The U.S. team won 19–8. Not until the London Games in 1948 did players play basketball indoors. Women competed for the first time in 1976.

In men's Olympic basketball twelve teams with twelve players may participate. Restrictions limit the number of teams from one continent. For example, North and South America are allowed two teams each, Europe may send four teams, Africa, Asia, Oceania, and the host country may send one team each. The two round robin draws eliminate all but four teams each, then those eight teams play each other in the quarterfinals to advance to the semifinal round and medal round.

For the first time, women's Olympic basketball will include twelve teams of twelve players each in 1996 at Atlanta. As the host country, the U.S. will compete, as well as, the World Champions in 1994, Brazil. Asia and Europe will each send three teams; the Americas will send two teams; Oceania and Africa will send one.

Strategy

Each team has five players, one center (usually the tallest player), two forwards, and two guards. Quickness and effective rebounding may give one team the added advantage, as well as the ability to switch from offensive plays to defensive plays. Defensive strategies include man-to-man or zone defense (not legal in the National Basketball Association [NBA]). The duration of the game is 40 minutes, twenty-minute halves and a ten-minute half-time.

A five-minute overtime is played to break any tie game. If a player shoots from beyond 20½ feet, three points are awarded his or her team; otherwise baskets count as two points, with the exception of free throws which count as one point.

Famous Basketball Champions in Olympic History

Jerry Lucas and **Oscar Robertson**   United States team; Rome, 1960.
Lucas and Robertson led the scoring with an average of seventeen points per game. Their team scored an average 102 points per game. Robertson won the NBA "Rookie of the Year" award in 1960–61; Lucas won the same honor in 1963–64.

Sasha Belov   Soviet Union; Munich, 1972.
Belov, a 6' 8" forward played in one of the most controversial games in Olympic basketball. With only three seconds remaining in the game, Belov received a long pass and made a basket to give the Soviets a 51–50 victory over the United States. The controversy arose over the extra three seconds the referee awarded the Soviets after two successful free throw shots by Doug Collins, an American. His shots put the U.S. in the lead. Because the clock showed only one second after Collins' free throws the American team protested the series of decisions that led to an additional three seconds for the Soviets. A committee heard the protests and ruled in favor of the Soviet team. To this day, the members of the 1972 U.S. team never collected their silver medals.

Drazen Dalipagic and **Dragan Kicanovic**   Yugoslavia; Moscow, 1980.
Dalipagic and Kicanovic led the Yugoslav team to a gold medal victory over Italy with an average of 24.4 points for Dalipagic and 23.6 points for Kicanovic.

Michael Jordan   United States; Los Angeles, 1984; Barcelona, 1992.
One of the most charismatic and well-known basketball players in the NBA today, Jordan helped the United States' Dream Team claim a 117–85 victory over Croatia in Barcelona. Professional basketball players were allowed to participate in the games for the first time in 1992. Jordan and his teammates beat their opponents by an average margin of 44 points per game.

Earvin "Magic" Johnson   United States; Barcelona, 1992.
One of the top basketball players in the NBA, winning five NBA titles in twelve seasons, Johnson teamed with Michael Jordan and other NBA professionals to make up the Dream Team. On November 7, 1991, Magic announced his retirement from basketball due to testing positive for the HIV virus. Despite having the AIDS virus, he joined the Dream Team in Barcelona and won a gold medal.

Iuliyana Semenova   Soviet Union; Montreal, 1976.
Iuliyana Semenova, a 6' 10½" athlete, who weighed 284 lbs., scored the most points during the 1976 Games with an average of 19.4 points and 12.4 rebounds per game. Surprisingly, she spent half the time on the bench.

Cheryl Miller   United States; Barcelona, 1992.
Miller averaged 16.5 points and 7 rebounds per game in Barcelona. She led the U.S. team to win the gold by beating their opponents by a margin of 28 points or more.

Further Reading

Benson, Michael. *Dream Teams*. Boston, MA: Little, Brown, 1991. 117 pp. Offers short clips of sports history and dream teams in a variety of sports. Reading level: 4th–8th grade.

Bird, Larry and John Bischoff. *Larry Bird's Basketball Birdwise*. Terre Haute, IN: Phoenix Projects, 1983. 144 pp. Though the photos are somewhat dated, Bird's basketball tips are excellent. Reading level: 4th–8th grade.

Gutman, Bill. *Michael Jordan*. New York: Pocket Books, 1991. 142 pp. Presents biographical information about Michael Jordan with photos. Reading level: 6th–8th grade.

Gutman, Bill. *Michael Jordan: Basketball Champ*. Brookfield, CT: Millbrook Press, 1992. 46 pp. Combines photos and brief chapters on Jordan's NBA career and lists his titles since playing in the NBA. Reading level: 4th–6th grade.

Morgan, Bill. *The Magic: Earvin Johnson*. New York: Scholastic Inc., 1991. 113 pp. Provides biographical information about Magic from his childhood to the present. Reading level: 4th–6th grade.

Novak, William. *My Life*. New York: Random House, 1992. 329 pp. In-depth biographical look at the life of Earvin "Magic" Johnson. Reading level: 6th–12th grade.

Basketball Activities and Discussion Questions

1. How Basketball Came To Be: Writing Assignment – Now that you have read the background on basketball, you have some ideas about how it came to be. Without any background information, imagine how a sport was originally invented. The Greeks invented stories to explain events even when they had no prior knowledge of the details. In three to five paragraphs, write a myth or legend about one of the sports below. Use details to describe and explain the origin of the sport. Include the person who invented the sport, the place, the reason, and how it was invented.

    How Football Came to Be   How Badminton Came to Be
    How Table Tennis Came to Be   How Judo Came to Be
    How Pole Vaulting Came to Be
    How Synchronized Swimming Came to Be

2. A Reader's Dream Team of Authors: The Men's Basketball Dream Team, made up of the best players in the top leagues of the National Basketball Association provided spectators with a once-in-a-lifetime event; they watched a superb group of talented and skilled athletes. Suppose you were asked, as a reader, to select twelve of the most outstanding authors in the world to become the Dream Team of Authors. The Dream Team of Authors must, as a group, write an outstanding story that surpasses all other stories. Rank the following elements of a story as being important in the selection process, then write the names of authors you would include on another sheet of paper.

    humor   setting   detailed description
    horror   conflict   dialogue
    sensory details obstacles   character development
    adventures   truth   a courageous hero or heroine
    plot   suspense

3. Sports Briefs: Check your school library or local library for a biography or sports almanac profile on one of the following Dream Team basketball players and give a brief (two to five minutes), but fascinating oral report on him.

    Earvin "Magic" Johnson   Christian Laettner
    Michael Jordan   David Robinson
    Larry Bird   Patrick Ewing
    Karl Malone   Scottie Pippen
    Clyde Drexler   John Stockton
    Chris Mullin   Charles Barclay

Learning Objectives: To demonstrate how inventive and innovative persons can create new sports. To choose a Dream Team of favorite authors and think about characteristics of highly skilled storytellers. To find out what type of skills and training a basketball player needs to be on the Dream Team.

Weightlifting

The ability to lift a tremendous weight has been linked to characteristically "strong men" for centuries. Through the oral tradition of myths, legends, and tall tales this association continued with references to Atlas, who carried the weight of the world on his shoulders, or Hercules, who strangled the two serpents in his crib as an infant.

Competitions in weightlifting took place in ancient Greece, but the first modern day version of the sport happened in the 1700s. Many of the Northern European countries such as Germany, Austria, Switzerland and Scandinavia held competitions.

Training clubs for weightlifting became popular in the 1860s. At that time the two-handed weights consisted of a metal bar between two balls. The balls were filled with sand, lead shot, or pieces of metal.

In the first modern day Olympic Games weightlifting included one— and two-handed lifts. By 1928, the one-handed lift was dropped. In two-handed lifts there were three categories, the press, the snatch, and the jerk. The press event was dropped from the Olympics in 1972.

Types of Weightlifting

Snatch Event Considered the more difficult of the two lifts, athletes must bend down and transfer the weight on the bar from foot level to above the head in one continuous motion. While the weight is above the head, the lifter may be in a crouched position. He must then stand straight up with the weight extended above his head. Once a down signal is given, the weightlifter may lower the bar.

Clean and Jerk The first phase of the lift called "the clean" is the movement of the bar from the platform (floor) to the shoulders. As in the snatch lift, the athlete may bend and squat under the weight to gain balance. The second phase called "the jerk" is the movement from the squatting position to an upright position. Simultaneously, the lifter pushes his arms upward and holds the weight with extended arms until the referee gives the down signal. Typically, more weight may be put on the bar in the clean and jerk event.

Famous Weightlifters in Olympic History

Norbert Schemansky United States; London, 1948 ; Helsinki, 1952 ; Rome, 1960 ; Tokyo, 1964 (445.0 kg).
Schemansky captured the gold medal by lifting 38 pounds more than his own world record. In all, he won four Olympic medals: one gold in the middle heavyweight division in 1952, a silver in the super heavy weight in 1948, and a bronze in 1960 and 1964 in the same division.

Rules in Olympic Weightlifting

Each competitor is given three chances to lift in each event. If a competitor wishes to break an Olympic record, he may be allowed a fourth attempt.

The lifter chooses the weight himself and between lifts, the weight must increase by increments of at least 2.5 kg. There is a time limit of 90 seconds for each individual lift or three minutes if the lifts are attempted in a row.

In the case of a tie, the lifter who weighs less is granted the top prize.

Three referees judge each lift watching for extra movements or instances of the bar touching the legs.

There are ten weightlifting classes.

Tamio "Tommy" Kono United States; Helsinki, 1952; Melbourne, 1956; Rome, 1960. Kono began weightlifting when he was fourteen years old. He and his family had been sent to a detention camp for Japanese Americans during World War II and it was during his stay at the camp that he became interested in the sport.

One of Kono's unusual qualities was his ability to compete in the Olympics in different weight classes. In the 1952 Games, he lifted in the lightweight class and won the gold. In 1956 he won the gold in the light heavyweight division. By 1960, he decided to lift in the middleweight division to compete against Aleksandr Kurynov. Kono failed to defeat his Soviet competitor and won the silver. Following his participation in the Olympics, Kono won the Mr. World Competition in 1954 and Mr. Universe competition in 1955 and 1957.

Yuri Vlassov Soviet Union; Rome, 1960; Tokyo, 1964.
Vlassov won the gold medal in 1960 with his first attempt in the clean and jerk event, lifting 185 kg. By the end of the competition, he dazzled the crowd by lifting 202.5 kg., breaking the world record. Following his successes in the Olympics, he retired from training to write poetry, something he had long dreamed of doing. Discouraged by his inability to find a publisher for his poetry, he returned to training for the 1976 Olympics and eventually won a silver in the super heavyweight division.

Vassily Alexeyev Soviet Union; Munich, 1972; Montreal, 1976.
Alexeyev's fame began two years before the 1972 Munich Olympics when he broke the world record in the three events of weightlifting. Three months later the combined total weight he lifted was 600 kg. That same year in the clean and jerk event he lifted 500 lbs.

At peak condition, Alexeyev weighed 337 lbs. A reporter once saw him order a breakfast of 26 fried eggs and a steak at a restaurant in Munich.

Alexeyev remained successful for many years. From 1970 to 1977 he broke 80 world records and was virtually the world's best weightlifter in the super heavyweight division for eight years. Each time he broke a world record, the Soviet government awarded him a monetary prize of between $700 and $1500.

Further Reading

Fahey, Thomas D. *Basic Weight Training for Men and Women*. Mountain View, CA: Mayfield Publishing, 1994. 170 pp. Helpful guide for those interested in weight training to improve strength and fitness. Reading level: 8th grade–Adult.

Schwarzenegger, Arnold and Charles Gaines. *Arnold's Fitness for Kids Ages 6-10*. New York: Doubleday, 1993. 122pp. Handy guide for parents, students, and teachers on fitness, motor skills, exercises and games related to fitness. Reading level: 2nd–6th grade.

Schwarzenegger, Arnold and Charles Gaines. *Arnold's Fitness for Kids Ages 11-14*. New York: Doubleday, 1993. 122pp. An overall guide to help young students learn about exercise, fitness, and nutrition. Reading level: 5th–8th grade.

Weightlifting Activities and Discussion Questions

1. Library Research: Look for the *Guinness Sports Record Book* or *Sports Almanac* in your school or local library to answer the following questions:

   a. The greatest amount of weight ever lifted by a man is _____ lbs.

   b. The greatest amount of weight ever lifted by a woman is _____ lbs.

   c. The youngest world champion weightlifter is _____.

   d. The oldest weightlifter in sports history is _____.

   e. The greatest overhead lift by a woman was _____ lbs.

   f. _____ won the most Olympic medals in weightlifting.

2. Strong Men: Pick one character from the following list to research. Read about the character and list the experience and adventures relating to strength and power; then present this information to your class in any form you choose, such as a poem or a dramatic performance, telling the story in a dynamic fashion, or in the first person as the character himself.

Hercules	Atlas	Samson
Paul Bunyan	Achilles	Superman

3. Steroid Use in the Olympics: In the 1988 Seoul Games two gold medalists from Bulgaria tested positive for drug use. Their medals were taken back and given to the second place finishers. Drug use has been so prevalent that more rigorous testing was initiated in 1988. One impact has been a reduction in the weights recorded in the 1991 world championships compared to 1988. Research the positive and negative effects of steroids on the body and discuss the sue and abuse of these drugs for weightlifters.

Learning Objectives: To use a reference source to find data. To explore the "strong man" motif that runs through literature. To debate the issue of drug use among Olympic athletes.

Answers to question 1: a. 6,270 lbs. by Paul Anderson in 1932. With his back he lifted a steel safe, which contained lead, and a variety of automobile parts. b. 3,564 lbs. by Josephine Blatt in 1895. c. Naum Shalamanov. At fifteen he became a world champion. d. Donat Gadonry, from Quebec, Canada. At 81 he lifted a 841 lb. barbell. e. 303 lbs. Karyn Tarter in 1985. f. Norbert Schemansky.

High Jump

The high jump was included in the six field events in the first modern Olympics in 1896. At that time, it was a standing high jump. Today, high jumpers may take a running approach and choose from a variety of styles.

Styles of High Jump

Scissors In the late 1800s and early 1900s high jumpers ran to the high jump horizontal bar and kicked one leg over at a time in a scissors-like fashion. The torso remained vertical for this type of jump.

Western Roll In 1912, George Horine used a new style of jumping called the western roll, and broke the Olympic record. Horine cleared the bar with his torso in a horizontal position and his knees together. Some western roll jumpers let their sides face the bar; others faced the bar with their bellies.

Straddle This is an offshoot of the western roll. In the straddle style one arm and leg precede the other arm and leg over the bar.

Fosbury Flop This style was named after Dick Fosbury, who won the gold medal in 1968. The jumper goes over the bar head first, with his back facing the bar.

Technique

Approach: Jumpers who use the Fosbury flop generally approach from 55' to 70' away and run in a curved path to the bar. Straddlers run from the side, usually taking seven steps before the take-off.

Take-off: Beginning about one arm's length away from the crossbar, straddlers lead with one foot, the leg and torso moving horizontal over the bar.

A jumper using the Fosbury flop pushes the leg closest to the bar toward the chest to get the upward movement for clearance.

Clearance: Straddlers roll over the crossbar sideways with the belly facing the bar. Floppers curl their bodies backwards over the crossbar leading with the head and shoulder blades.

Famous High Jumpers in Olympic History

Mildred "Babe" Didriksen United States; Los Angeles, 1932.
One of the greatest female athletes in history, Didriksen tied with Jean Shiley (United States) at a height of 5'5 ¼" (1.657 m). Both jumpers attempted 5'6" and missed. Because Babe Didriksen used the western roll style the judges called it illegal and gave Shiley the gold. Didriksen proved to be far ahead of her times in technique; the western roll has become an accepted style for high jumping.

The Rules

The objective in the high jump is to clear the horizontal bar that is set at various heights held by two upright posts. The jumper is allowed two misses, on the third miss, he or she is eliminated.

A miss may be counted as hitting the bar so it falls to the ground.

The high jumper with the fewest misses wins in the event of a tie.

Technically, the high jumper must take off from one foot, but there have been a few exceptions to this rule.

The thickness of the shoes a jumper uses is limited to an inch (13 mm) for the sole, and ⁷⁄₁₀ths of an inch (19 mm) for the heel.

Cornelius Johnson United States; Berlin, 1936.
Johnson easily won the gold medal by setting a new Olympic record of 6'8"
(2.03 m). The United States captured all three medals; besides Johnson's gold,
David Albritton won the silver, and Delos Thurber won the bronze. Adolph Hitler
left the stadium before the medals ceremony, although he had stayed to congratulate the winners of the other events. Johnson and Albritton were African Americans.

Walter Davis United States; Helsinki, 1952
Davis jumped ½" more than his own height to win a gold medal. He was 6'8" tall and
weighed 206 lbs. When he was eight, he had polio, and for three years, he could not
walk. By the time he reached college, he was an All-American basketball player.

Dick Browning United States
Even though he did not participate in the Olympics, his unusual style of clearing
7'6" (2.28 m) dazzled audiences. He somersaulted over the crossbar.

Valery Brumel Soviet Union; Rome, 1960; Tokyo, 1964.
Brumel won the silver medal in 1960 and the gold medal at the Tokyo Games. In
1964 he broke the Olympic record by clearing the crossbar at a height of 7'1"
(2.18 m). One year later, Brumel was involved in a motorcycle accident that nearly
severed his right foot. His high jumping career and popularity fizzled. John
Thomas was one of the high jumpers who competed against Brumel in the 1964
Games. Learning of the accident, Thomas sent Brumel a telegram encouraging him
to return to high jumping. Five years later Brumel did, but he never reached the
international level of competition. Instead he earned a Ph.D. in sports psychology
and wrote a novel on scientists.

Iolanda Balas Romania; Melbourne, 1956; Rome, 1960; Tokyo, 1964.
In the 1956 Games, Balas placed fifth. However, after this experience she won 140
high jump competitions in a row, spanning over a ten and a half year time period.
She became the first woman to clear 6'. In 1961, she high jumped 6'3". She won the
gold medal in both 1960 and 1964.

Gary Chamberlain United States
Another high jumper with an unusual and noteworthy style, Chamberlain did a
back handspring over a bar 7'4" high.

Richard Fosbury United States; Mexico City, 1968.
Fosbury's new high jumping technique revolutionized the sport. The technique
carries his name, the Fosbury flop. In 1968, Fosbury set a new Olympic record by
clearing 7'4". By 1980 a majority of the Olympic high jumpers were using the
Fosbury flop style of jumping.

Further Reading

Diagram Group, *The Sports Fan's Ultimate Book of Sports* Comparisons. New York: St.
Martin's Press, 1982. 192 pp. Fascinating comparisons of sports in every category.
Reading level: 3rd-8th grade.

Matthews, Peter. *Guinness Track and Field Athletics: The Records.* Great Britain:
Guinness, 1986. 175pp. Informative guide on the records and brief profiles of
several superstar athletes in track and field events. Reading level: 4th-Adult.

Equipment
The uprights
stand 13'3" (4 m)
apart with
supports holding
a crossbar
weighing
approximately 4.4
lbs. (2 kg).

High Jump Activities and Discussion Questions

1. Using library resources and reference books such as the *Guinness Track and Field Athletics* make a chart of the heights high jumpers have cleared over the past 100 years. You may want to create a graph or chart on a computer program or display the actual heights in a classroom hallway.

2. Mentally, Olympic athletes must jump tremendous obstacles to compete and perform at their highest potential. Choose one of the athletes on the following list and try to discover the motivation he or she had to clear the obstacles to success, mentally and physically.

    Jim Abbott - (Born without a right hand)

    Jesse Owens - (Race discrimination)

    Wilma Rudolph - (Polio)

    Lis Hartel - (Polio)

    Károly Takács - (Loss of his right hand)

    Greg Louganis - (Dyslexia, Race discrimination)

    Jim Thorpe - (Race discrimination)

3. The Olympic motto comes from a Latin phrase Baron Pierre de Conbertin heard used to describe the achievements of students at Arcueil College where he taught. In Latin it is *Citius, altius, fortius,* meaning "swifter, higher, stronger."

    Skimming through Olympic record books in virtually any event, this motto rings true. As class activity, choose one event and trace the changes in times, distances, or throws over the 100 year time span,

    OR   Test the motto in other areas of technology, by researching the following products and inventions. Present the history of the product with a visual display of the technological changes, an actual product demonstration, or an advertisement tracing the changes. Be imaginative! Here are some ideas for consumer products or equipment:

Cars	Microwaves	Medicines
Airplanes	Synthesizers	Camcorders
Rockets	Radios/Walkmans	Computers
Military Weapons	Trains	Records/Cassettes/CDs
Televisions	Video Recorders	
Telephones	Bicycles	

Learning Objectives: To compare high jump heights from each decade. To consider the mental preparation needed to succeed in competitive sports. To learn the Olympic motto and apply it to a consumer product or equipment.

Football (Soccer)

Variations of the game of soccer can be traced to 80 B.C. in China when players kicked a ball through a goal of two bamboo poles stretching 30 feet in the air. Greeks and Romans played a similar game using a ball filled with hair. Italians created a game called *"calcio"* in which the players carried, kicked or passed a ball beyond a goal line. Stories from Roman legend claim the Romans kicked around skulls of defeated soldiers for recreation and the sport of soccer grew from this legend.

In England soccer became popular in the twelfth and thirteenth centuries. At that time the soccer field included the downtown section of a village. Storefronts and homes were sometimes damaged while players moved the ball through the streets toward the goal.

In 1863, the modern game of soccer became standardized with the formation of the Football Association in England. Many of the rules established at that time are still part of soccer rules today. Entering the Olympics in 1900, soccer was the first team sport. Today it is one of the most popular sports in the world.

The Game of Soccer

The dimensions of a soccer field are 74 yd. (68 m) wide by 114 yd. (105 m) long. The goals are 8' high and 24' wide. Each team plays with eleven players. The halves are 45 minutes long. The team that controls the ball the most usually wins the competition.

Positions

Goalie (Goalkeeper) He may use his hands to block any shots in the 192-square foot area right in front of the goal.

Fullbacks These are four or five defensive players who prevent the opponents from scoring.

Halfbacks Sometimes called midfielders, they are ready to make plays or shift to a defensive stance on the field.

Forwards The main objective of the forwards is to score goals. They may be called wings or strikers.

Strategy

Depending on the country and the alignments, the backs and forwards for many teams may be grouped as a four-two-four or four-three-three or four-four-two defensive setup.

Famous Soccer Players in Olympic History

Giampiero Combi Italy; Paris, 1924; Amsterdam, 1928.
One of the best goalkeepers in Italy, Combi helped the Italian team win the bronze medal in the 1928 Olympic Games.

Jose Leandro Andrade Uruguay; Paris, 1924; Amsterdam, 1928.
Part of the gold medal winning team in 1924 and 1928, Andrade played right half-back. His agility, positioning ability, and juggling skills made him an idol in Uruguay. He also competed in the first World Cup in 1930. Mysteriously, the Uruguayian team won the gold two years in a row but never competed in Olympic soccer again.

Joszef Bozsik Hungary; Helsinki, 1952.
As a tremendous passer and playmaker, Bozsik became one of the greatest halfback wings in Europe in the 1950s. He led the Hungarian team to win the gold medal in 1952. In 1958 he played center forward in the World Cup.

Romario Brazil; Seoul, 1988; Barcelona, 1992.
In the final game of the 1988 Games, Romario scored the only goal for Brazil's team. They lost to the Soviet Union 2-1. After the Olympics, Romario played in the Netherlands for five years. During that time he scored 98 goals. His attacking skills as forward rank him as one of soccer's top players.

Michelle Akers United States
Though Akers has not competed in an Olympic soccer game, she is a hopeful for the 1996 Olympics in Atlanta. She plays on the United States national team which won the Women's World Championship in China in 1991. Her ten goals during the tournament and outstanding performance led the U.S. Soccer Federation to name Akers the Female Athlete of the Year.

Further Reading

Arnold, Caroline. *Soccer*. New York: Franklin Watts, 1991. Introduces the basics of soccer technique and rules. Reading level: 3rd–5th grade.

LaBlanc, Michael L. and Richard Henshaw. *The World Encyclopedia of Soccer*. Detroit, MI: Visible Ink Press, 1994. This in-depth encyclopedia on soccer includes biographical profiles of the game's top players in history, descriptions of soccer organizations with their addresses throughout the world, and rules of the game. Reading level: 6th grade–Adult.

Soccer Activities and Discussion Questions

1. Spelling and Word Search Activity: The following words could be used as a spelling lesson for one week. Using graph paper make your own word search puzzle using the following soccer terms:

soccer	striker	forward	free kick
bend	offside	shin guards	boot
halfback	overhead kick	fullback	goalie
corner kick	penalty	challenge	goal kick

2. Even though Edson Arantes do Nascimento (Pelé) never participated in the Olympics his skill and tremendous attitude influenced thousands of soccer players. He once admitted, "I have an extra instinct for the game. Sometimes I can take the ball and no one can foresee danger. And then, two or three seconds later, there is a goal. This doesn't make me proud, it makes me humble, because it is a talent that God gave me." (Littlefield, 26)

   Read the chapter on Pelé in the book *Champions: Stories of Ten Remarkable Athletes* by Bill Littlefield aloud or as a class; then discuss the following questions:

   Why do you think Pelé has become such an influential personality in the game of soccer?

   Though Pelé had only attended school through 4th grade he tutored himself to challenge his intellect and to improve his performance as a soccer player. Name two ways he challenged himself.

   After doing the readings, discuss the mental attitude he brought onto the field and how it added to his successes. Can you name other sports heroes who present similar attitudes on the soccer field, basketball court, tennis court or football field?

3. Some would claim that soccer is the most popular sport in the world. If popularity is based on the number of participating countries and the number of viewers, soccer would be ten times greater in popularity than the Super Bowl in the U.S. At the same time, the emotional intensity has caused violent and tragic results. In small groups, research the following violent incidents that caused upheaval in homes and stadiums.

   Berlin, 1936 In the game between Peru and Austria the Peruvian fans became so angry they attacked an Austrian player. What happened to the Peruvian team?

   Tokyo, 1964 In the qualifying match for the Olympics held in Lima, Peru, a riot broke out leaving 328 people dead. Explain the details of this horrible tragedy.

   El Salvador, 1968 An 18-year old soccer fan shot herself because her team (El Salvador) lost to Honduras in a World Cup competition. The President of El Salvador and the entire soccer team attended her funeral.

Learning Objectives: To introduce soccer terminology to students. To read about one of the most influential persons in soccer history. To discuss some of the tragic and unexpected happenings at soccer matches.

Diving

Phases of a Dive

Approach

Takeoff

Elevation

Execution

Entry

Diving began as an offshoot of gymnastics in the 1600s. Swedish and German gymnasts trained by practicing their flips and somersaults on apparatus over water. Gradually, more people tried the sport and it evolved into a separate sport from gymnastics. The English held diving championships in 1893. The Olympic Committee added diving to the list of sports included in the Games for the first time in 1904.

There are two events in the diving competition for men and women—platform diving and springboard diving. The platform is 33' high (10 m) just about the height of a three story building; it is stationary. The springboard is 10' (3 m) above the water, and there is springiness and flex to the board. Similar to gymnastics in its aesthetic appeal, diving has an element of danger to it. A Soviet diver hit his head on the concrete platform in 1983 and died a week after the accident from head injuries.

Seven judges award scores for each diver in Olympic competition. Men and women in the springboard and platform events must perform required dives. Added to the standard requirements are points for the degree of difficulty to the dive. When each individual diver completes his turn, the seven judges award a score from zero to ten for the execution, two scores are eliminated and the other five are multiplied by the degree of difficulty of the dive.

Phases of a Dive

Approach This first phase begins as soon as the diver is ready to take the first step. A minimum of three steps must be taken before the diver reaches the end of the board. Judges look for smoothness and dynamic energy.

Takeoff Judges look for a diver with confidence, control, and smooth transitions from the approach to the hurdle, the final step of the approach to the takeoff.

Elevation Generally, the more height a diver can attain, the more time there is to execute the movements.

Execution Proper technique combined with overall form and artistic beauty make up this phase.

Entry Judges place an emphasis on two criteria related to entry: First, the angle at which the body enters the water, and second, the amount of splash—the least amount is preferable.

Famous Divers in Olympic History

Greg Louganis United States, Montreal, 1976; Los Angeles, 1984; Seoul, 1988.
Born to fifteen-year-old parents, one Samoan and one Swedish, Louganis was adopted as an infant. He suffered many hardships as a child. Because his skin was darker, he was teased by other children; and because he was dyslexic he learned more slowly. After he turned four, his parents took him to dance and gymnastics lessons, and he continued until the day they found him doing acrobatic stunts off the backyard pool diving board.

Louganis' first experience in Olympic competition took place when he was only sixteen. He won the silver medal in Montreal. He missed the 1980 Games due to the boycott. In 1984 he competed in both the springboard and the platform events.

For the final dive of the platform competition, Louganis chose a triple somersault in a tuck position, the dive with the highest difficulty points. In divers' circles, it is called the "dive of death." Louganis had witnessed a Soviet diver a year earlier hit his head on a platform and plunge into the pool unconscious, dying a week later. Louganis paused and dove with grace and precision. One judge gave him a perfect ten. He won the gold in both the platform and the springboard competitions.

Four years later in Seoul, Korea, while Louganis dove in the preliminary round for the springboard event he hit his head on the diving board. His first reaction to the incident was embarrassment, then it was fear. He knew he had acquired the AIDS virus and did not want anyone else to be at risk. Meanwhile, his doctor stitched his cut and Louganis went back in the line-up to dive. He thought his chances to advance in the medal round were completely lost, but he would not give up. He paused to begin his dive—the audience's silence made him nervous. Louganis put his fist to his chest and imitated how fast his heart was beating. Everyone laughed. The tension left the room and Louganis dove. He qualified for the final round and won the gold for the second time in a row.

In the platform event, Louganis and Xiong Ni, a Chinese competitor, were contenders for the gold. Louganis' last dive was the triple somersault in tuck position, the "dive of death." With exceptional poise and skill, he performed superbly. He became the first diver to win the gold in both the platform and springboard competitions in two consecutive Olympics.

Klaus Dibiasi Italy; Tokyo, 1964.
Klaus Dibiasi's father, Carlo, participated as a diver in the 1936 Olympics. He coached his son. Klaus practiced with tremendous determination, at times diving between 130 and 150 dives a day for six out of seven days a week. He won the gold in the platform event in 1968, 1972, and 1976. In 1964 he won a silver in platform, and a silver in the springboard event in 1968.

Pat McCormick United States, Helsinki, 1952; Melbourne, 1956.
McCormick won four gold medals; two in 1952 for the platform and springboard events, a feat she repeated in 1956. She gave birth to a son only eight months prior to the Melbourne Games, but continued to train by swimming at least a half mile per day up until two days before his birth.

<u>Maxine "Micki" King</u> United States; Mexico City, 1968; Munich, 1972.

Micki King placed fourth in Mexico City. She was in first place until her ninth dive. When she executed the dive, she broke her forearm when she hit the springboard. As a result, she lost her first place lead. In Munich, King gained the first place position after her eighth dive. Her final dive for the competition was the same reverse one and a half somersault with a one and a half twist she attempted when she broke her forearm four years earlier.

Further Reading

Louganis, Greg and Eric Marcus. *Breaking the Surface.* New York: Random House, 1995. 290 pp. Highlights the Olympic performances in 1984 and 1988 and traces Louganis' life from his childhood to the present. Reading level: 6th grade–Adult.

Sandelson, Robert. *Swimming and Diving.* New York: Crestwood House, 1991. 48 pp. Explains the swimming distances and events in the Olympics and spotlights outstanding Olympic swimmers. Reading level: 4th–8th grade.

American Red Cross. *Swimming and Diving.* St. Louis, MO: Mosby Lifeline, 1992. 354 pp. In depth and informative guide on all aspects of swimming, safety, and diving. Color photos and drawings included. Reading level: 5th grade–Adult.

Diving Activities and Discussion Questions

1. There are six different classification for dives in competition. Choose the dive on the right that you think fits the classification on the left.

   Classifications

   Dives

   1. Diver faces the water and dives forward.

   a. Armstand Somersault

   2. Diver faces the platform and dives backward.

   b. Reverse 1½ Somersault

   3. Diver faces the water, but dives backwards.

   c. Forward Double Somersault

   4. Diver faces the platform and dives forward.

   d. Flying Back Somersault

   5. Diver must add a twist to the dive.

   e. Back 1½ Somersault 2½ Twists

   6. Diver performs a handstand before diving. (Platform diving only)

   f. Flying Inward 1½ Somersault

2. Read aloud a chapter from Greg Louganis' autobiography *Breaking the Surface*. I would suggest "The Ninth Dive" or "Seoul 1988." Do these accounts fit with your expectations about athletes competing in the Olympics?

3. Discussion Question: The shock Greg Louganis' experienced from hitting his head on the springboard in the preliminaries went beyond his physical injury. He was HIV-positive and the doctor stitching his head did not know about his HIV status. Do you think the Olympic Committee should require all athletes regardless of the events in which they participate, to answer health related questions about the possibility of having HIV or AIDS?

Learning Objectives: To review the classifications for competitive diving. To talk about AIDS testing for Olympic athletes.

Answers to question 1: 1.c. 2.d 3.b 4.f 5.e 6. a.

Special Olympics

The beginning of the Special Olympics tradition started with a simple conversation between Mrs. Eunice Kennedy Shriver and a friend. The friend asked Mrs. Shriver if she could recommend a summer camp for a person who was mentally retarded. Mrs. Shriver knew nothing about such camps, and when she researched the possibility, discovered that none existed. Her response to this discovery was anger and action. In 1963 Mrs. Shriver, her husband Sargent Shriver, and 100 volunteers held a five-week day camp for persons with mental retardation, the location was in the Shriver's backyard in Rockville, Maryland.

Horseback riding, archery, tennis, volleyball, swimming, and gymnastics were some of the activities available to the campers. After the five-week camp session, Shriver began thinking of an Olympic-type competition for children with mental retardation. In 1968 Anne McGlone, a worker for the Chicago Park District asked Mrs. Shriver and the Kennedy Foundation to sponsor a Special Olympics in Chicago. On July 20, 1968 at Soldier Field in Chicago, 1,000 persons with mental retardation competed in the first Special Olympics. At that time the events were limited to track and field and swimming. Twenty years later, with organized chapters for Special Olympics in every state and 73 countries, the International Olympic Committee gave the Special Olympics official recognition. Six thousand athletes competed in the Eighth International Summer Games in 1991.

Special Olympics Outstanding Athletes

Jenny Skinner Equestrian

Jenny Skinner has participated in the Special Olympics for twelve years in swimming, cross-country skiing, and equestrian events. In 1989, she received the Spirit of Friendship Award. She was an alternate for the equestrian team in the 1991. If she is not riding horses herself, she likes to assist younger boys and girls in learning how to ride. "I ride three days a week and sometimes I can help with the little kids,"[1] she said. Her coach Larry Herschler praised her achievements, "Jenny's dedication and enthusiasm are a true representation of the spirit of Special Olympics."[2] When Jenny is not riding horses or training for the Olympics, she enjoys being with her family and friends and occasionally gives talks about special education to interested teachers. One of the benefits of the Special Olympics for Jenny is her eagerness to reach out to the community.

Brian F. Loeb Swimming

When Brian was an infant his mother thought he was developing normally. But after several months, it became apparent that Brian's ability to process ideas and thoughts was much slower than his older brother. Brian's mother became ill with polio in the first few months of her pregnancy, and she was paralyzed and confined to a wheelchair as a result. As a young boy, Brian rarely talked and because of his mental retardation, other boys teased him at school.

When Brian was fourteen, he decided to participate in a swimming event in the Special Olympics for the first time. It took an entire minute for him to swim one length, but the reward was an Olympic medal. To be a winner made Brian feel incredible; his confidence changed so much that he talked more freely and felt more comfortable around other people. Loeb's achievements inspired his paralyzed mother to set a goal to walk by herself. On the very day Brian turned eighteen, he swam in the 25-yard freestyle and won the gold. As he stepped out of the pool, the spectators started to sing "Happy Birthday" to him. Overcome by the emotion and her son's accomplishment, Mrs. Loeb stood up on her own two feet for the first time in eighteen years! Then she joined the spectators by singing "Happy Birthday."

The Special Olympics, "taught us that it isn't the strength of your body or mind that counts—it's the strength of your spirit,"[3] Mrs. Loeb said in an interview about her son. At 38, Brian had competed in the Special Olympics for twenty-three years. During that time he won 62 gold medals, six silver, and two bronze in swimming, floor hockey, downhill and cross-country skiing, and bowling. In the international competitions, he won two gold medals and three silver.

Brian has supported himself as a maintenance man for the past five years and through the Screen Actor's Guild has acted in one movie and three commercials.

Further Reading

Brown, Fern. *Special Olympics*. New York: Franklin Watts, 1992. 64 pp. Offers background on how the Special Olympics began and how it is organized. Reading level: 3rd–5th grade.

Reed, Kevin. *A Season for Dreams*. Saratoga Springs, NY: Chowder Press, 1989. 152 pp. A fictional story of about a dying man and a boy overcoming tremendous obstacles as a Special Olympian. Reading level: 5th–8th grade.

Wartski, Maureen Crane. *My Brother is Special*. New York: Dutton, 1981. 137 pp. A fictional story of a mentally retarded boy and his sister's efforts to help him participate in the Special Olympics. Reading level: 7th grade–Adult.

Bueno, Ana. *The First 25 Years: Special Olympics*. San Francisco, CA: Foghorn Press, 1994. 174 pp. Presents the beginnings and growth of the Special Olympics and highlights individual participants. Reading level: 5th–8th grade.

Notes

1. Bueno, Ana. *The First 25 Years: Special Olympics*. p.143.

2. Ibid., p. 143.

3. Ibid. p. 140.

Special Olympics Activities and Discussion Questions

1. Guest Speaker: Invite a guest speaker to talk about the Special Olympics. If your community does not have a local chapter representative, check with the state chapter or write to: Mrs. Eunice Kennedy Shriver, Special Olympics International, 1350 New York Avenue NW, Suite 500, Washington, D.C., 20005. Prepare for the guest speaker by creating at least ten thoughtful questions about the Special Olympic events or athletes and learning what the following terms mean:

   Cerebral palsy   Disabled

   Educable   Mental retardation

2. Special Olympic Pen Pal: Let each student write one letter to a potential Special Olympic Pen Pal. Send the letters to a state chapter or the Washington address above. Write a cover letter to suggest a possible pen pal exchange with a group of Special Olympic athletes. Students may include information about sports they enjoy, favorite subjects in school, favorite authors, foods they like, pets, and other interests. Also, add questions for the person receiving the letter.

3. As a class project, read a fictional novel on the Special Olympics and discuss the obstacles and benefits of participating in the events.

   Rank the following traits in the order of importance for a Special Olympic athlete, one being the most important, ten being the least important.

   ____courage   ____family support

   ____spirit   ____physical stamina

   ____determination   ____creativity

   ____problem-solving abilities   ____dreams

   ____positive mental attitude   ____money

   ____self-confidence   ____will power

Learning Objectives: To learn more about the participants in the Special Olympics.

Cycling

Cycling events are divided between track events that take place on a wooden, circular track and road events which may vary between five and twenty-five miles in length.

Cycling began with the invention of the first bicycle in Paris by Comte de Sivrac. His 1791 model was designed with wooden wheels, a wooden bar stretching to the seat, and no pedals. Persons sitting on this bicycle propelled it by pushing off the ground first with one leg then the other. Several variations of this model bicycle were created for racing and transportation. By 1834 a Scottish man named Kirkpatrick designed a new version complete with pedals and rods connecting to the main moving mechanisms.

During the early part of the 1900s and the 1920s, cycling became extremely popular in the United States. Chicago hosted the first World Championships in 1893. Worldwide cycling participants competed in the first Olympic Games in 1896. Within seven years the first Tour de France bicycle race, a cross-country event, offered another opportunity for international competition. Since that time the Tour de France has become one of the most challenging cycling races of all time. Cycling in Europe has continued to be popular since the first Tour de France competition. In the United States, interest in cycling decreased with the invention of the automobile, but it was restored during the 1980s when people used bikes for recreation and to conserve energy.

Track and Road Events

The track race takes place in a velodrome, which is a wooden track approximately 333.3 meters in circumference. The ends of the track are banked at an angle of about 33 degrees. Red and green flashing lights give the racers and the spectators an indication of which racer is in the lead. Women competed in the match sprint track event for the first time in 1988.

Bicycles used in the track events generally have only one gear and no brakes.

Track Events

Match Sprint Racers are timed for a 200-meter distance.

Individual Pursuit Two racers compete against each other attempting to either pass the opponent (each racer starts at opposite ends of the velodrome), or ride faster than the opponent.

Team Pursuit Similar rules to the individual pursuit except four racers are involved. The race is finished when the fastest team's third cyclist crosses the finish line or the third racer catches up to the third racer of the other team.

Points Race Racers must complete a course of 100 laps, approximately 40 kilometers. The object is to score the most points by lapping the field.

Kilometer Time Trial Racers ride as fast as possible for 1000 meters. Pacing and stamina are critical to this race.

Road Events

Individual Road Race Depending on the city where the Olympics are held, this race may be five miles or up to 25 miles long. Even though it is the individual who wins this race, teams may help each other through "drafting" (a strategy in which one rider rides directly behind another to save energy). The rider in back may save up to 25 percent of his energy, using it later to become the front cyclist or to win the race in the final stretch.

Individual Time Trial Riders compete alone against the clock. Men usually race 45–55 kilometers, women race 25–35 kilometers.

Mountain Biking Events

Mountain biking will be in the Olympics in 1996. Men and women will compete in a cross-country race on a course of forest trails, gravel roads, and varied terrain for a distance of between four and twenty miles.

Equipment

Many cyclists choose bicycles that are lightweight but strong enough to endure rugged races. Track bicycles have one gear, but no brakes, while road bicycles may have up to fourteen gears and brakes.

Famous Cyclists in Olympic History

<u>Rudolph "Okey" Lewis</u> South Africa; Stockholm, 1912.
Lewis started the 199-mile (320 km) road race at 2:00 a.m. He led the race at the 120 km. mark by 11.5 minutes and 17 minutes at the 200 km mark. His final time 10 hours, 42 minutes and 39 seconds was eight minutes faster than the second place racer.

<u>Russell Mockridge</u> Australia; London, 1948; Helsinki, 1952.
Mockridge gave up cycling several times, then returned as many times because he was a top competitor. Even though he did not win a medal in the 1948 Games, he won two gold medals two years later in the British Empire Games. He followed this victory with a gold in the 1000-meter time trial and a gold in the tandem with Lionel Cox as his partner.

<u>Daniel Morelon</u> France; Tokyo, 1964; Mexico City, 1968; Munich, 1972; Montreal, 1976.
 Morelon won a total of five Olympic medals throughout the years he competed—two golds, a silver, and a bronze in the sprint and a gold in the tandem with Pierre Trentin.

<u>Steve Hegg</u> United States; Los Angeles, 1984.
Even though Hegg was not favored to win a medal in the 4000-meter individual pursuit, he finished eleven seconds in front of the other 32 cyclists after the qualifying round. The test of Hegg's endurance arrived when he raced Rolf Golz from Germany. Hegg won the gold with a time of 4:39:35 over Golz. Some believe Hegg's outstanding performance arose from blood boosting a week before the final race.

Women competed in road events for the first time in 1984.

Custom-made bicycles made with titanium or other thin seamless metal tubing may cost $4,000 to $7,500.

Blood boosting involves extracting some of the racer's blood, freezing it, then reinjecting the blood again into the body to raise the hemoglobin level. This process is believed to increase the athletes endurance level before a race.

Connie Carpenter-Phinney United States; Los Angeles, 1984.
Connie Carpenter-Phinney finished seventh in the 1500-meter speed skating event in the 1972 Winter Olympic Games when she was only fourteen. After an ankle injury, Carpenter switched from speed skating to cycling; she also tried rowing before returning to cycling. During the 1984 competition, Carpenter found herself behind Rebecca Twigg, another American cyclist. About three meters from the finish line Carpenter caught up to Twigg and threw her bike forward when she came near the finish line to capture the gold by only a half a wheel.

Carpenter recalled the victory in her book, *Training for Cycling*. She said that it was "not until the next day when I saw the tape of the finish of my race on television did I really know how close the finish was. Only inches. All those years and all that hard work for a few inches."

Further Reading

Hinault, Bernard and Claude Genzling. ***Road Racing***. Brattleboro, VT: Vitesse Press, 1988. 208 pp. Hinault has won the Tour de France five times in addition to other world championships. His expertise and training advice is presented clearly and informatively for cycling enthusiasts. Photos included.

LeMond, Greg and Kent Gordis. ***Complete Book of Cycling***. New York: G.P. Putnam's Sons, 1987. 352 pp. Written by the 1986 Tour de France champion, this book includes practical advice about choosing bicycles, maintenance tips, and stories about the Tour de France from an expert racer.

Phinney, Davis and Connie Carpenter-Phinney. ***Training for Cycling***. New York: Perigee Publishing, 1992. 254 pp. Includes training tips on techniques, nutrition, racing tactics, and bicycle handling for competitive cycling. Reading level: 6th grade–Adult.

Porter, A.P. Greg LeMond, ***Premier Cyclist***. Minneapolis, MN: Lerner Publs., 1990. 64 pp. Biographical account of LeMond's cycling career. Reading level: 4th–6th grade.

Cycling Activities and Discussion Questions

1. Conduct an Interview: As a class project or school newspaper assignment conduct an interview with an athlete or a panel of athletes. Here are some suggestions for conducting an interview:

   1. Try to read or find out information about the athlete through a library resource (books, almanacs, magazines, etc.) or other persons.

   2. Write out five to ten questions you might ask the athlete.

   3. Select the question that might encourage a story or lead to other questions first.

   4. Be spontaneous. If you think of another question after listening to an answer, ask that question. When you interview it is important to let the person you are interviewing know you are listening attentively.

   5. Take notes.

   6. If you want to take a direct quotation, double check the statement, so you know it is written the way the person meant it to be written.

   7. The overall meaning is what you want to capture, it is more important than writing the exact words.

Here are some interview questions and responses between Connie Carpenter-Phinney (gold medalist in the cycling road race) and myself:

February 9, 1996
Interview with Connie Carpenter (Cycling Gold Medalist in the road race event in 1984)

ML: In your book *Training For Cycling* you reflected on your experience at the Olympics saying, "Not until the next day when I saw the tape of the finish of my race on television did I really know how close the finish was. Only inches. All those years and all that hard work for a few inches." Do you think the victory was worth all the training, discipline, and effort?

CC: I trained because I loved the sport, the opportunity to travel, and the experience let me escape from a normal teenage life.

ML: What was your training schedule like when you were thirteen years old?

CC: When I was in the seventh grade I went to school on Mondays, drove from Madison to West Allis to train on the 400-meter oval on Tuesday, stayed in West Allis through Thursday and returned to school again on Fridays. Sometimes I would have to wake up on Saturday at 5:30 a.m. to race in West Allis. If I traveled to Holland or Norway, I would take my school books along and study my lessons between training sessions. Typically, I trained twice a day during four days a week and once a day the rest of the week.

ML: After you competed in the 1972 Winter Olympics at age 14 what direction did you want to take?

CC: I wanted to become the world champion within a couple years. I later realized how naive I was. As an athlete I realized how hard it was to advance from being *good* at a sport to being *great* at a sport. It was an eye-opening experience.

ML: When you injured your ankle and could not compete in the 1976 Olympics, how did you feel?

CC: I was crushed, devastated, I had no other plans. It was a lesson to me to always have a back-up plan. You find out who your friends are when things are not going well. My family supported me and my brother, Chuck introduced me to cycling.

ML: What are the benefits of being an Olympic gold medalist?

CC: You can make a living off of something you love. You can be creative in your work.

ML: What kinds of experiences do you want to pass along to your children?

CC: What is important is variety and exposure to a lot of different sports and the opportunity to choose. My parents were not all that athletic, but they exposed me to figure skating and gymnastics as a girl and supported me. It is important to know where the drive is coming from. If it is from the parents, it may not last.

ML: Are you doing anything related to cycling these days?

CC: Davis (her husband) and I are running bike camps in the summer in Colorado with an emphasis on road and recreational biking. It is our eleventh year of summer camps. Otherwise, I like to Nordic ski in the winter, hike and mountain bike in the summer. If you are interested and fourteen or older, write to: Phinney-Carpenter Bike Camps, Box 252, 2626 Baseline Rd., Boulder CO 80303 (1-303-442-2371).

2. Cycling in the Tour de France: In small groups, research at least one aspect of the Tour de France and give a brief but informative presentation as if you are in the event. Try to include at least one or two visual charts, pictures, maps, or photos to make the presentation memorable. Use atlases, almanacs, magazines or books for resources.
Possible Research Groups:
   • Map of the course, distance, miles per day, French spectators.
   • Nutrition during the race, calories burned.
   • Training before the race, endurance test.
   • Energy necessary to race each day.
   • Bicycles that are the most efficient and aerodynamic.
   • Winners like Greg LeMond–Tour de France

3. Is blood boosting legal or safe? Discuss or write an essay on whether blood boosting should be allowed in Olympic competitions. Many cyclists have used this method in the recent past. Lasse Viren was accused of blood boosting in 1976 after winning the 10,000 meter running event in Montreal.

Learning Objectives: To learn some tips on conducting an interview. To research the Tour de France. To discuss and write an essay on blood boosting.

Gymnastics

The sport of gymnastics dates back to ancient Greece; it was also popular in other parts of the world such as China, Persia, and India. At that time it was introduced to prepare men for battles and to perfect the shape of their bodies. It comes from the Greek word *gymnos* meaning naked. In ancient times the gymnasts performed the exercises in the nude, even in public facilities. During the eighteenth century the Germans grew interested in the sport. They used a variety of new pieces of equipment, including: climbing poles, ropes, balance beams and ladders. Friedrich Jahn added the use of parallel bars and rings and created ideas for routines on the horizontal bar. By the late 1800s gymnastic clubs became extremely popular in Europe. Gymnastics was one of the sports included in the first modern Olympics in 1896. Men competed in individual, combined individual and team events as early as the 1924 Olympics in Paris. Women could compete in 1928 in only a team combined exercise. Twenty-four years later, five individual events were added: the combined, balance beam, floor exercise, uneven bars and horse vaults.

Categories of Gymnastics

While men compete exclusively in artistic events, women can compete in one rhythmic event. **Artistic gymnastics** involves doing a routine on a balance beam or parallel bars. **Rhythmic gymnastics** involves using various props such as ropes, hoops, or ribbons which become part of the routine. For instance, a gymnast may jump through a hoop or wave a ribbon while leaping into the air. The coordination of body movement and use of the ribbons or hoops is one of the areas judges observe. Judges for artistic gymnastic routines look at the difficulty of moves (some are compulsory) and the artistic beauty of the combination of movements. If a gymnast loses her balance, fails to include the required moves, performs longer than the allotted time, or gives a weak execution, points may be deducted from her score. Women begin with a score of 9.40, men start at 9.00.

Types of Apparatus

Floor Exercise Women usually combine dance movements, tumbling skills, and balances with music for a floor exercise routine. Men typically string together multiple *saltos* (flips and somersaults), twists, and tumbling skills without musical accompaniment. Smooth transitions and grace are key elements of the floor exercise.

Vault Using a piece of equipment called a horse (4' high for women, 4½' for men), the gymnast sprints to the launching board and performs twists or tucks while vaulting over the horse. The men's vault is in line with the launching board, the women's horse is set perpendicular to the board.

Pommel Horse Men's competition only. Using the pommel horse apparatus tests the strongest of male gymnasts because for most of the routine he is using only one hand. The horse is 5' long (1.5m), 4' high (1.2m), and 14" wide (35cm). Judges look for smooth, quick, fluid swinging, scissoring movements in the legwork.

Still Rings Men only. Two fiberglass rings are hung 8½' (2.6m) above the floor by leather or nylon straps. In this event, judges test the gymnast's skill by the stillness of the rings. Precision in body movement is crucial too.

Parallel Bars Men only. The equipment consists of two parallel wooden or fiberglass bars set 6' (1.8m) above the ground. Routines include balances, two-second holds, saltos, and a dismount.

Horizontal Bar Men only. In this event, gymnasts strive to combine swinging movements, flips, twists, and release moves (leaving the bar momentarily) without pausing or stopping. The flexible hollow, steel bar is set 8½' (2.6m) above the mats.

Uneven Bars Women only. Women perform routines on two wooden or fiberglass bars, one set at 8' (92.4m), the other is set at 5' (1.5m) above the floor. Each gymnast must include a minimum of ten moves, no more than four can be executed on one bar in a row. Like the horizontal bar the gymnast uses swings, release moves, pirouettes, and hand stands.

Balance Beam Women only. Dance movements, flips, balances, tumbling moves, mounts, and dismounts must be performed on a 16' long (4.87m), 4" wide (10.2cm), wooden beam covered with vinyl or leather. The gymnast has only 70–90 seconds to complete the entire routine.

Famous Gymnasts in Olympic History

Olga Korbut Soviet Union; Munich, 1972.
Olga Korbut's enthusiasm, smiles, determination, and spectacular performances during the 1972 Olympics charmed adults and children throughout the world. In the United States alone, the number of girls signing up for lessons in gymnastics increased from 15,000 before the Games to over 50,000 by 1974. She won two gold medals in the balance beam and floor exercise, and a silver in the uneven parallel bars. After her successes at the Olympics, she traveled to the United States. On one occasion when she met President Nixon, she recalls the tremendous compliment he gave her, "He told me that my performance in Munich did more for reducing the political tension during the Cold War between our two countries than the embassies were able to do in five years."[1]

Shun Fujimoto Japan, Montreal, 1976.
Fujimoto participated in the team competition during the Montreal Games. Six individual gymnasts make up a team. When the scores are tabulated, the points awarded for the medal are based on the top five highest scores. During Fujimoto's floor exercise routine he accidentally fractured his knee cap. Without showing any signs of pain or injury, he advanced to the next event without saying a word to his coach or teammates. He received a 9.5 on the pommel horse. Thinking about the

third event, the rings, Fujimoto worried, "I knew that if my posture was not good when I landed I would not receive a good score. I must try to forget the pain."[2] Fujimoto completed the routine and the dismount from eight feet in the air with a crisp finish, but shortly after his feet landed, his knee buckled and he felt an excruciating pain. His coach and teammates knew he should not continue. Without their teammate, the Japanese team had to give nearly perfect performances to win. They handled the pressure easily and won by a margin of 40/100ths of a point.

Nadia Comaneci Romania; Montreal, 1976.
She was first woman to score a perfect 10.0 in gymnastic competition. By the end of the week she had scored seven perfect 10.0 scores. She won three gold medals, one silver, and one bronze, all at the age of fourteen!

Mary Lou Retton United States; Los Angeles, 1984.
Retton became the first American to win the gold in the individual all-around competition (uneven parallel bars, balance beam, vault, and floor exercise). At sixteen, the Olympic Games gave her the first opportunity to compete against athletes from other nations. Bela Karolyi, her coach, had coached Nadia Comaneci in the Montreal Games in 1976. Tied for first with Ecaterina Szabb, of Romania, Retton had to perform perfectly on the vault. And she succeeded, scoring a perfect 10.0.

Dominique Dawes United States; Barcelona, 1992.
Dawes became the first African-American gymnast to win two silver medals in the world championships held before the 1992 Olympics. She won a bronze at Barcelona. Her formula for success began at age nine when she prepared for a gymnastics met by writing the word DETERMINATION in crayon on her bedroom mirror. As she matured, she added two words to the formula: dedication and dynamics. She is a hopeful for the 1996 Olympics in Atlanta.

Further Reading

Jones, Betty. *Wonder Women of Sports*. New York: Random House, 1981. 69 pp. Presents twelve outstanding women athletes, including Nadia Comaneci, Babe Didrikson, Wilma Rudolph and others. Reading level: 3rd–6th grade.

Levy, Elizabeth. *Go For the Gold*. New York: Scholastic Inc., 1992. 182 pp. Fictional novel about a young girl preparing to compete in the gymnastics event in the Olympics. Reading level: 4th–6th grade.

Miklowitz, Gloria D. *Nadia Comaneci*. New York: Grosset and Dunlap, 1977. 90 pp. This biographical account traces the selection and training of Nadia Comaneci, as well as the highlights from the Olympic competitions. Reading level: 4th–6th grade.

Tatlow, Peter. *The World of Gymnastics*. New York: Atheneum Publishers, 1978. 128 pp. This informative book written by experts in the world of gymnastics covers the routines and movements of gymnasts competing in every possible event. Illustrations and photos included.

Notes
1. Greenspan, Bud. *100 Greatest Moments in Olympic History*. Los Angeles, CA: General Publ., 1995, p. 92
2. Ibid., p. 49.

Gymnastics Activities and Discussion Questions

1. Personal Narrative Writing Assignment: Each of the Olympic gymnasts could write his or her own story about participating in one or several events. Fujimoto might write about the pain of his broken kneecap. Comaneci might remember the thrill of the perfect 10.0.
   Write your own personal narrative (a true story about your own life). Here are some questions to guide you.

   • Who are some special people in your life?

   • Have you ever visited a place that made you uncomfortable or thrilled?

   • What are your favorite activities in your leisure time?

   • What are your least favorite activities?

2. Discuss the ages of most gymnasts. Why do you think it is so important to train at a young age and compete at age fourteen, fifteen or sixteen?

3. Vocabulary Enrichment: Define the following terms used in gymnastic events, then illustrate the definition by drawing the word in a formation similar to the definition.

giant	kip	pike position
pirouettes	salto	arch
flip	handspring	layout
straddle	twist	tuck
aerial		

Learning Objectives: To write a personal narrative. To discuss the age factor in training for gymnastics. To learn vocabulary terms related to gymnastics.

Water Polo

Developed during the 1860s in England, water polo was also called "football in the water" or "aquatic soccer." Resort owners in England created the game to draw guests to their establishments. The earlier version of the game consisted of barrels, paddles and a ball. The team members sat on the wooden barrels and used the paddles to move the ball around the water. With this kind of equipment the game became hazardous. Once the barrels and paddles were eliminated the ball and goal remained as the main pieces of equipment. Even though the water polo players swam in water just above wading level, the underwater kicking, punching, dunking, and pushing caused many injuries and near drownings. In the 1920s two changes made a tremendous impact on the sport. First, the dimensions and depth of the pools were expanded, requiring more advanced swimmers. Second, the Hungarian team introduced a more efficient method of passing the ball so it would not come close to touching the water.

Rules of the Game

Seven players make up a team. The goalie, the drivers (similar to forwards in basketball), defenders, and the hole-man (comparable to the center in basketball) who plays close to the opponent's goal.

A player may only use one hand to touch or throw the ball.

A player may not use a clenched fist to score.

Players may not touch the sides or bottom of the pool, except the goalie. Substitutes may enter the pool after a goal, after a third foul, or during the breaks between periods.

The duration of a match is broken into four periods lasting seven minutes. There are two minute breaks between each period.

Fouls

Minor fouls like touching the bottom or sides of the pool or holding a ball underwater results in losing possession of the ball.

Penalty fouls such as using two hands to throw the ball or using a clenched fist results in a free penalty shot by the opposing team.

Exclusion fouls may include kicking an opponent underwater or splashing water in an opponent's face. This results in a free throw and removal of the player for 45 seconds or until a goal is scored.

Dimensions of the Playing Area

The length of the pool is 33 yd. (30 m) and 22 yd. (20 m) wide. The depth of the pool is approximately 5'11" (1.8 m).

The objective of water polo is to pass the ball to team members to try to score by throwing the ball in the opponent's goal.

A Memorable Incident in the Olympic History of Water Polo

Melbourne, 1956. Hungary vs. Soviet Union

Just three weeks prior to the Melbourne Games in 1956, the Soviet Union sent 200,000 soldiers across the Hungarian border to crush an anti-Communist movement. To protest the brutality and deaths, many countries refused to compete in the Games. Surprisingly, Hungary and the Soviet Union competed. The water polo match between these countries reflected the bitterness and violence happening in Hungary.

Hungary had dominated the water polo competitions for years and their dominance carried on throughout this match. They led 4–0 into the fourth period. At one point, a judge spotted blood spilling into the pool from a group of swimmers. A Soviet player slashed one of the Hungarian players named Ervin Zador under his left eye. Zador was ushered out of the pool. Meanwhile, the Hungarian spectators left their seats ready to start a fight with the Soviet team.

Police officers calmed the crowd while the judges held a conference about the match. They decided to stop the match and grant Hungary the victory. The Hungarians won the gold medal with an undefeated record.

Further Reading

Frommer, Harvey. *Olympic Controversies.* New York: Franklin Watts, 1987. 128 pp. Fascinating chapters on the controversies happening in the Summer and Winter Olympics, such as the case of Jim Thorpe being stripped of his gold medals and the Nazi influence on the Berlin Games. Reading level: 5th grade–Adult.

Wallechinsky, David. *The Complete Book of the Olympics.* New York: Penguin, 1988. 687 pp. Comprehensive listings of the medalists in every Olympic sport since 1896, plus anecdotes about the athletes or the incidents that take place. Reading level: 5th grade–Adult.

Water Polo Activities and Discussion Questions

1. As a class project, research the two countries involved in the water polo match, Hungary and the former Soviet Union. You may use encyclopedias, atlases, almanacs, or books as resources. Create your own booklet on the particular country. As an example, you may want to look at a book entitled *Learning to Swim in Swaziland* by Nila K. Leigh which describes daily experiences in Swaziland from an eight-year-old's perspective.

   Try to include at least ten of the following topics in the booklet. Include only one topic on a page. Illustrate the pages to make the booklet more colorful. Then you may bind the books together with yarn or other binding materials and display them in your school library.

   Topics
   1. Flag
   2. Education
   3. Sports and Games
   4. Food (Recipe)
   5. Historic Places or Landmarks
   6. Size and Population Comparisons (in relation to a U.S. state)
   7. Traditional Dress
   8. Unusual Expressions and Customs
   9. Currency
   10. Folktale (Brief)
   11. Famous People
   12. Maps: products & neighboring Countries

2. Compare and contrast communist political systems with democratic political systems. Highlight countries with communist governments on a world map. Use current resources and indexes from the library.

3. Choose one of the former Soviet Republics below; read about the country, and create a travel brochure highlighting the features of the landscape, history, literature, architecture, or sites. Photocopy pictures to illustrate the brochure. Fold the paper, so it opens as a brochure.

Russia	Ukraine	Estonia	Tajikistan
Belarus	Uzbekistan	Armenia	Kyrgyzstan
Kazakhstan	Georgia	Moldova	Latvia
Azerbaijan	Turkmenistan	Lithuania	

4. Using Harvey Frommer's *Olympic Controversies* read and discuss the fifth chapter, "The Olympics of the Cold War Years." Related to this issue of the Cold War, talk about the reasons the Soviet Union and the United States boycotted the Olympics in the summers of 1980 and 1984.

Learning Objectives: To study the countries of Hungary and the Soviet Union. To compare communist political systems with democratic political systems.

Tennis

Due to the controversy about the eligibility of professional athletes in the competition, tennis was absent from the Olympics for 64 years. It has regained its status as an Olympic sport, and it now attracts top athletes. Most competitors today are ranked in the top 40 in the world and must have competed in the men's international team competition, the Davis Cup, or the women's equivalent, the Federation Cup.

Dating back to ancient Greek and Roman times, tennis became popular in France when a minstrel introduced it to the French Court in the tenth century. Playing tennis served as recreation for monks in their cloisters in the eleventh century. The early form of tennis was called *jeu de paume,* or sport of the palm. Equipment consisted of a handmade ball paddled back and forth with the hands. The game also involved a simple net stretched from one end of the room to the other for indoor play. A mound of dirt served as the net in outdoor play.

Louis IV banned tennis, thinking it undignified. Despite this setback, the popularity of tennis spread throughout France and Great Britain. By the sixteenth century the French considered it their national game. At that time in Paris, 1000 tennis courts were available for enthusiastic players.

In 1873, Major Walter Wingfield of England introduced an adapted version of tennis with an hourglass-shaped court and net that was 7' high. Eventually, the All-England Croquet Club learned about Wingfield's game, adapted the rules to open-air lawn tennis, and held a tournament in 1877, the first Wimbledon lawn tennis championships.

Mary Outerbridge introduced the sport to the United States and the first court was built at the Staten Island Cricket and Baseball Club in 1874. The first U.S. Open tournament was held in 1881.

Equipment

Racquets consisting of a graphite or composite frame and gut or synthetic gut strings are most popular today. Tennis balls are neon yellow in color and filled with air pressure for more bounce and responsiveness.

Strategy

To hold one's serve in tennis is crucial in singles and in doubles, for the server has a one shot advantage over his opponent. The receiver needs to successfully return the serve, and "break" the server. The server wins a game if he wins four points in a row or wins by two points. The first player to win six games wins the set. All the Olympic matches are two out of three sets except the finals; they are three out of five sets for the men. Players will play off for the bronze medal.

Olympic tennis

The **singles** competition allows 64 men and 64 women to compete.

The **doubles** draw allows 32 teams for women and 32 teams for men.

Famous Tennis Champions in Olympic History

Suzanne Lenglen France; Antwerp, 1920.
Lenglen was considered one of the greatest tennis players of her time. She won the gold medal in ten sets, only losing four games during the entire competition.

Steffi Graf Germany; Seoul, 1988; Barcelona, 1992.
Steffi Graf won the gold medal in women's singles in 1984 when she was only fifteen. At that time, tennis was listed as a demonstration sport. After beating Martina Navratilova in the French Open in 1987, Graf became the No. 1 ranked player in the world. The following year she won the Grand Slam, a term that describes four major international tennis tournaments—the Australian Open, French Open, Wimbledon, and the U.S. Open. Only one week after beating Sabatini in the U.S. Open and becoming the fourth woman ever to win the Grand Slam, Graf competed in the Olympics in Seoul. She met Sabatini again in the finals, winning in two sets, 6-3 and 6-3 for her "golden" grand slam! In 1992, Jennifer Capriati met Graf in the finals and for the first time upset Graf 3-6, 6-3, 6-4 to win the gold.

Mary Joe Fernandez and **Gigi Fernandez** United States, Puerto Rico; Barcelona, 1992.
Mary Joe and Gigi Fernandez won the first set in a suspenseful final match against Spain's home team of Arantxa Sanchez Vicario and Conchita Martinez. The latter team raised the level of their performance just after the unexpected arrival of King Juan Carlos and Queen Sophia. They rallied to win the next five games and the set. Unfortunately for the Spainards, the royal influence did not last and Vicario and Martinez lost 2–6 in the third set. Fernandez and Fernandez won the gold.

Marc Rosset Switzerland; Barcelona, 1992.
Rosset served 33 aces in the finals to beat the Spaniard Jordi Arrese.

Monica Seles United States
Even though Seles has been absent from the professional circuit for two years, she is a hopeful competitor in Atlanta in 1996. On April 30, 1993, a German named Guenther Parche stabbed her in the back to remove her from the top ranking in the world and from competition with Steffi Graf. Although the decision to play professional tennis again has been a difficult one for her, Seles played in the U.S. Open in 1995 and lost to Graf in the finals.

Further Reading

Groppel, Jack L. *High Tech Tennis*. Champaign, IL: Human Kinetics, 1992, 223 pp. Technical guide with updated information on stroke production and proper equipment for tennis players. Reading level: 7th grade–Adult.

Hilgers, Laura. *Steffi Graf*. New York: Time Magazine Co., 1989. 119 pp. Starting with Graf's appearance in the 1988 Olympics, this book covers her achievements through 1988 as a world-class tennis player. Reading level: 4th–6th grade.

Tennis Activities and Discussion Questions

1. Tennis vocabulary: Choose seven words and use a dictionary to find at least two meanings for each word. Then write a limerick or a riddle using some of the words below.

    Example: *There once was a fellow named Ace,*
    Who played tennis like it was a race,
    At his turn to serve,
    He never lost nerve,
    But sometimes he fell on his face.

ace	love	tennis
advantage	overhead smash	chip
break point	poach	trajectory
crosscourt shot	serve	lob
deuce	set	volley
fault	slice	gut
groundstrokes	topspin	

2. Is new technology helping the game of tennis? One of the latest controversies in tennis circles is a question of technology. Should there be a limit to the materials used for tennis rackets and the size of the head, whether it is an oversized racket or a wide body? Some claim that the game has changed considerably with the technological improvements in tennis rackets. Check the *Reader's Guide to Periodical Literature* for magazine articles on new improvements in tennis rackets. Prepare your own opinion about the issue and debate whether rackets should have limitations or no limitations. Would it be fair to set up an international code of design for tennis rackets so the players have similar equipment?

3. Where would you draw the line in allowing amateur or professional athletes in an Olympic sport? The main reason tennis was excluded from the Olympic Games for 64 years was a difficult decision involving professional and amateur athletes. Why would it be important to exclude professionals? Are there sports that would not exist in world competition without the professional athletes? What is the advantage of keeping amateur athletes involved in Olympic competitions?

Learning Objectives: To become familiar with tennis terminology. To discuss technological improvements in racket design. To think about the changes in Olympic competition when professional athletes are allowed to compete.

Team Handball

Team handball was invented in Denmark about the same time and for the same reasons basketball was invented in the United States. Danish athletes were looking for a way to stay in shape during the cold winter months, so they developed a soccer-type game using hands instead of feet. It eventually turned into the sport, team handball. A Danish man named Holger Nielsen set up the official rules and began organizing games in 1906.

In 1936, team handball became an Olympic sport. At that time, the teams played with eleven players on a side and the matches took place outdoors. Even though the Scandinavian countries did not participate in the 1936 Games, they still competed indoors in their own countries, training with a seven player team on each side instead of eleven. For indoor international tournaments, most teams agreed to allow only seven players per team. Later this number became official for all competitions including the Olympics.

Rules of the Game

The object of team handball is to work the ball down the court by passing and running, in order to throw the ball into the goal to score. The team with the highest number of points wins.

Only the goalie is permitted to play in the goal area line, unless an offensive or defensive player leaps in the air and crosses the boundary line. Once he lands in the goal area, he must return to the outside court without touching the ball.

Seven players compete for two 30-minute halves. Players are allowed to play anywhere on the court except inside the goal area. The offense usually consists of two wings and a circle runner; defense consists of left and right backcourt players and a center.

During the course of passing the ball to teammates, a player may run three steps or hang onto the ball for up to three seconds. Dribbling is acceptable for as long as a player wishes, but it is not as common in team handball as it is in basketball.

As a method of blocking a shot or an opponent, a player may come between the goal and the ball with his body. If he uses his hands to push or trip an opponent, a free throw is awarded the opponent or if the pushing is more serious the player is sent out of the game for two minutes.

Equipment

The court dimensions are 131' (40m) in length and 65.5' (20m) wide. The goal area line is six meters from the goal. The goal dimensions measure 7' (2m) X 10' (3m). The ball 23" in circumference for men (60cm) and 22" (56cm) for women.

Similar to basketball, the team that uses quick passes, fakes, and screening to score will be tougher competitors.

Team Handball Medalists in Olympic History

MEN'S WINNERS

1936
Gold–Germany
Silver–Austria
Bronze–Switzerland
1972
Gold–Yugoslavia
Silver–Czechoslovakia
Bronze–Romania
1976
Gold–Soviet Union
Silver–Romania
Bronze–Poland
1980
Gold–East Germany
Silver–Soviet Union
Bronze–Romania
1984
Gold–Yugoslavia
Silver–West Germany
Bronze–Romania
1988
Gold–Soviet Union
Silver–South Korea
Bronze–Yugoslavia
1992
Gold–Unified Team
Silver–Sweden
Bronze–France

WOMEN'S WINNERS

1976
Gold-Soviet Union
Silver–East Germany
Bronze–Hungary
1980
Gold–Soviet Union
Silver–Yugoslavia
Bronze–East Germany
1984
Gold–Yugoslavia
Silver–Republic of Korea
Bronze–People's Republic of China
1988
Gold–South Korea
Silver–Norway
Bronze-Soviet Union
1992
Gold–South Korea
Silver–Norway
Bronze–Unified Team

Further Reading

Jennison, Keith W. *The Concise Encyclopedia of Sports*. New York: Franklin Watts. 1970, 165 pp. Contains clear descriptions of a wide variety of sports played around the world. Though team handball is not included, rugby and cricket are included in this encyclopedia. Reading level: 6th grade–Adult.

Diagram Group. *The Sports Fan's Ultimate Book of Sports Comparisons*. New York: St. Martin's Press, 1982. 192 pp. This outstanding resource for sports enthusiasts provides visual illustrations and charts comparing similar sports and lesser known sports. It would be an excellent resource for libraries. Reading level: 4th grade–Adult.

Team Handball Activities and Discussion Questions

1. Similar Sports: Compare and contrast the game of team handball to basketball and soccer using sports reference books in the library. Set up a chart with three columns comparing the similarities and differences. Read about cricket and rugby, two sports that are very similar to baseball and football. Find out what the rules are for these games.

2. American Handball - Another game called handball became popular in the United States in the 1960s. Check your library for a sports encyclopedia and read about this very different kind of handball. Clue: Two to four persons played this sport. What sport, still played today is an offshoot of this game?

3. Update on Yugoslavia - Since 1991, Yugoslavia has changed its borders dramatically and has been a focal point for world attention. Read about the history of Yugoslavia and the new republics: Croatia, Slovenia, Bosnia and Herzegovina, and Macedonia. Check your local newspaper for current happenings in Bosnia. Talk about the presence of United States troops in Bosnia at this time. What are the causes of the conflicts in this region of the world?

Learning Objectives: To learn to use library resources to compare team handball to other team sports popular in other parts of the world. To conduct a study on the conflicts in Bosnia and trace the history of Yugoslavia using recent publications.

Baseball

Some pitchers throw fast balls at 98 mph (157 kph).

Baseball originated in Hoboken New Jersey in 1846. An umpire named Alexander J. Cartwright arranged and supervised the first game after creating the rules. Since that time, the popularity of the sport has spread throughout the United States and 60 different countries in the world. Baseball became an Olympic sport for the first time in 1992. It was previously demonstrated at St. Louis in 1904, at Stockholm in 1912, in Berlin during 1936, Helsinki in 1952, Melbourne in 1956, Tokyo in 1964, Los Angeles in 1984, and Seoul in 1988.

Eight Olympic baseball teams play a round-robin tournament to determine the medal winners. Each team may include twenty players. The eight teams must win the championships in their respective continent to win a berth in the Olympics. In 1996 the United States team will automatically compete since the U.S. is the host country.

The Field and the Players

The diamond of bases measures 90 square feet. Directly 60'6" in front of home plate is the pitcher's mound. The pitcher may throw up to 100 pitches in one game. He attempts to strike out a batter with a variety of pitches like the curve ball, fast ball, slider, sinker, or knuckler.

The Game

Each team competing attempts to score the most home runs in a nine-inning game by hitting the pitched ball strategically and running all four bases. While the batting team attempts to score, the nine players in the infield and outfield attempt to put the batters out before they score any points. Once the batting team has three outs their opponents switch from outfield to infield and they have a chance to score.

Strategy

Teams with strong hitters rely on them to score winning runs. Another alternative to big hits is outfoxing the opponents by stealing bases or bunting.

Famous Baseball Players in Olympic History

Jim Abbott United States; Seoul, 1988.
In the final game, the United States played Japan. Jim Abbott, the twenty-one-year old pitcher from Flint, Michigan pitched the entire nine-inning game and led the U.S. team to a 5-3 victory to win the gold. One of the most incredible stories about Jim Abbott is he achieved success, despite the fact that he was born without a right hand. His ability to pitch and field a ball developed when he was a boy.

Besides playing catch with his father, he used to throw a ball against a wall with his left hand, shift his glove to his left hand to catch it, then take the glove off again to throw it back to the wall. When he was a boy, Abbott pictured himself as a professional baseball player. He remembers dreaming about playing, never sure how many hands he had in the dreams. His dreams came true in 1988 when he signed a contract with the California Angels. After playing with the Angels for four years, he pitched for the New York Yankees for two years. In 1995 he returned to play for the Angels.

Further Reading

Gutman, Bill. *Jim Abbott Star Pitcher*. Brookfield, CT: The Millbrook Press, 1992. 48 pp. Follows Abbott's baseball career from his boyhood to his professional career with the California Angels. Reading level: 3rd-6th grade.

Sloate, Susan. *Hotshots Baseball*. Boston, MA: Little, Brown, 1991. 116 pp. This *Sports Illustrated* book for kids offers interesting stories about baseball stars like Lou Gehrig, Mickey Mantle, Sandy Koufax, and Jim Abbott. Reading level: 5th-10th grade.

Sullivan, George. *Sluggers: Twenty-Seven of Baseball's Greatest*. New York, NY: Atheneum, 1991. 74 pp. Presents the all-time batting records and backgrounds of the best in baseball's history.

Walker, Paul Robert. *Pride of Puerto Rico the Life of Roberto Clemente*. Orlando, FL: Harcourt Brace Jovanovich, 1988. 136 pp. Features a biographical account of the great baseball hero, Roberto Clemente. Reading level: 5th-8th grade.

Baseball Activities and Discussion Questions

1. Using the list below, choose ten words and write a dramatic newspaper article. Remember to include answers to the five questions (Who? What? When? Why? Where?).

ball	grand slam
strike	bullpen
batting average	earned run
bunt	sacrifice
error	foul ball
pinch hitter	steal
fly ball	earned run average

2. It's Your Choice: One of the reasons many baseball players in the United States have not participated in the Olympics is because the Olympic Games overlap with the baseball leagues' regular season. The other reason is professionals were not allowed to compete in the Olympics. Now that the restrictions for professionals are changing in basketball and tennis, professionals may also be invited to play baseball. If baseball could be included in the winter Olympics, the professionals would not have to interrupt their season. Here is a list of all-time outstanding players. Select a dream team of nine plus a designated hitter to play an imaginary game. You will notice some players are no longer living, but this is a chance to dream, right? If you like, you may add extra players, too.

Baseball's Dream Team

Jose Canseco	Reggie Jackson
Eddie Matthews	Nolan Ryan
Micky Mantle	Roberto Clemente
Willie Mays	Rod Carew
Lou Gehrig	Joe Di Maggio
Babe Ruth	Jimmie Foxx
Hank Aaron	Stan Musial
Jackie Robinson	

3. Using library resources, research one of the players in the list above or a favorite player not found on the list. Prepare a list of ten significant incidents in this player's life to place on an overhead transparency. Examples might include: childhood experiences, developing a skill, watching a star baseball player, keeping track of baseball statistics

   When you have read at least three books on the person and think you are ready to answer the questions you prepared, ask your classmates to interview you as though you are the famous baseball player you researched. For example: To Hank Aaron - Do you hold the record for the most home runs in baseball history?

Learning Objectives: To write a newspaper article using baseball terms. To set up a dream team of baseball players. To research a baseball player's life.

Beach Volleyball

Atlanta's Demonstration Sport. The popularity of beach volleyball has spread from the sandy beaches in Southern California in the forties to beaches throughout the world in the last twenty years. This popularity has led to the selection of beach volleyball as a demonstration sport for Atlanta's 1996 Olympics.

With the help of corporate sponsors and television coverage, players may earn up to six-digit salaries with the winnings from tournaments. The first official beach volleyball tour happened in 1976. The prize award at that time amounted to $5,000, not including travel expenses. In 1987, Rio de Janeiro hosted the first World Championships of Beach Volleyball. For the first time on television, spectators watched teams from eight different countries competing for the world title. That same year, the Federation Internationale de Volleyball started to lobby for acceptance of beach volleyball as an Olympic sport. Years later, the Olympic Committee agreed to include beach volleyball with full medal status for only one year.

Like indoor volleyball, the first team to win fifteen points wins the game. If the game is tied at fourteen all or fifteen all, the teams must win by two points. Most matches are three out of five games in indoor competitions.

Teams

In preparation for the Games in Atlanta, team players from over 50 countries will play in several Federation Internationale de Volleyball tournaments to determine the top ranked teams. Only twenty-four men's teams and sixteen women's teams will participate in the Olympics.

Strategy

With only two players per team, both players must be skilled in all the fundamentals of the game. They must serve, bump, set, smash, block, and dig with exceptional accuracy. At the same time, players must balance their strengths and weaknesses in skills with slower movement due to running barefoot in sand. Jumping for smashing or blocking requires earlier preparation than indoor volleyball, since the explosive vertical jumping power is decreased in sand. Players may use the wind or sun as factors to win points especially on the serve. Jump serves are commonly used to score points against the opponents or to force errors.

Favorites in the Beach Volleyball Competition

Roberto Lopes Da Costa and Franco Neto Vieira Brazil
Da Costa and Vieira are a top-ranked beach volleyball team that will be competing in Atlanta.

Sandra Pires and Jacqui Silva Brazil
In the Federation World Series tournaments held in 1995 and 1996, this women's team is a possible gold medal winner.

Karch Kiraly and **Kent Steffes**   United States
Kiraly won two gold medals playing indoor volleyball. Kiraly and Steffes have played off and on as a team since 1990. In 1992 they won sixteen out of nineteen tournaments, including a streak of 13 tournaments in a row. They will be a favorite team for the United States.

Common beach volleyball slang terms

Ace - A serve that hits the opponent's sand without any player on that side touching it.

Block - To counter the smash, both hands are raised above the net in the position where the smash is coming over the net.

Bump - The return of serve. Both arms must be held together when using two hands to contact the ball.

Dig - Usually a diving defensive shot in response to the smash.

Dink - A looping short shot over the blocker's hands.

Jump Serve - The server takes a running jump then serves the ball.

Kill - An offensive smashing unreturnable shot following a set.

Rainbow - A gentle shot over the opponents landing near the back line.

Shank - A bad pass or dig.

Sideout - A term used when the receiving team prevents the serving team from scoring a point. The receiving team earns the serve.

Spike - To hit the ball as hard as possible into the opponent's court.[1]

Further Reading

Nelson, Rebecca and Marie J. MacNee. *The Olympic Factbook*. Detroit, MI: Visible Ink Press, 1996. 855 pp. This detailed book is a spectator's guide to the 1996 Summer Games. It gives the history of each event, highlights from Barcelona, and medalists from past Olympics. Reading level: 6th grade–Adult.

Ontario Science Centre. Illustrated by Pat Cupples. *Sportworks*. Toronto, Canada: Centennial Centre of Science and Technology, 1989. 96 pp. Provides more than 50 short explanations of science experiments related to sports. Reading level: 5th grade–Adult.

Notes

1. Nelson & MacNee. The Olympic Factbook. p. 727–728.

Beach Volleyball Activities and Discussion Questions

1. Surface Shuffle: Have you ever played baseball on grass, then on pavement? In many cases, the nature of a sport may change drastically or slightly depending on the playing surface. Beach volleyball players have an added challenge performing on sand in their bare feet. In the chart below, change the "normal" surface of the sports listed to a new and inventive surface.

Sports	Surfaces
_____ football	mud
_____ soccer	snow
_____ basketball	water
_____ hockey	jungle floor
_____ baseball	conveyor belt floor
_____ golf	gravel
_____ motorcycle racing	ice
_____ running	trampoline flooring

2. Was tug-of-war in the Olympics? The following is a list of demonstration sports that were discontinued. In small groups, write a list of reasons why these sports were discontinued. If you are not familiar with the sport, be sure to look it up in the library. You may want to research the correlation of the sport and the time period it was introduced.

   Cricket, 1900 Paris   Rackets, 1928 London
   Croquet, 1900 Paris   Roque, 1904 St.Louis
   Golf, 1900 Paris; 1904 St. Louis   Rugby, 1900 Paris;
   Jeu De Paume, 1908 London   1908 London
   LaCrosse,1904 St. Louis; 1908 London   1920 Antwerp
   Motor Boating, 1908 London   1924 Paris
   Polo, 1900 Paris; 1908 London
    1920 Antwerp; 1924 Paris; 1936 Berlin   Tug Of War 1900-1920

3. Sports Played 'Round the World: Explore sports that are popular in different countries in the world. Choose from the list below or introduce one you have discovered in a reference or resource book, or learned about from newspapers or television.
   • Kite-flying (India, South America, Thailand, Japan)
   • Snowsnake (Canada, Native Americans)
   • Octopush (South Africa, Canada)
   • Tossing the Caber (Scotland)
   • Sepak Takraw (Malaysia)

Learning Objectives: To strengthen library research and reading skills by introducing students to sports that have been discontinued in the Olympics. To explore sports played in different countries in the world.

Selected Bibliography

Aaseng, Nate. *Great Summer Olympic Moments*. Minneapolis, MN: Lerner, 1990. 71 pp. Presents fourteen chapters on record-breaking and medal winning Olympic champions. Reading level: 4–8th grade.

———. *World-Class Marathoners*. Minneapolis, MN: Lerner Publications, 1982. 80 pp. Provides background on the history of the marathon and seven great marathon runners. Reading level: 2nd–6th grade.

Barry, James P. *The Berlin Olympics*. New York, NY: Franklin Watts Inc. 1975. 86 pp. In-depth look at the 1936 Berlin Olympics, especially the African Americans response to Nazi propaganda. Reading level: 5–8th grade.

Diagram Group. *The Sports Fan's Ultimate Book of Sports Comparisons*. New Y‹ St. Martin's Press. 1982. 192 pp. This book contains intriguing displays and charts comparing sports in similar categories. Reading level: 3rd- Adult.

Frommer, Harvey. *Olympic Controversies*. New York: Franklin Watts, 1987. 128 pp. Gives an insightful perspective on the controversies connected to the personalities and political climate during the summer and winter Olympic competitions. Reading level: 6th grade–Adult.

Gentry, Tony. *Jesse Owens*. New York: Chelsea House, 1990. 112 pp. Biographical account of one of the greatest track stars in Olympic history. Reading level: 6–8th grade.

Greenspan, Bud. *100 Greatest Moments in Olympic History*. Los Angeles, CA: General Publishing, 1995. 224 pp. This oversized treasure of anecdotes about Olympic athletes is inspiring and highly recommended for school libraries. Reading level: 6th grade–Adult.

Gutman, Bill. *Michael Jordan*. Brookfield, CT: Millbrook Press, 1992. 48 pp. Biographical sketch of Michael Jordan, including highlights from his NBA career. Reading level: 2nd–6th grade.

Hollander, Phyllis. *100 Greatest Women in Sports*. New York: Grosset and Dunlap, 1976. 142 pp. Organized according to categories of sports, this excellent resource describes the lives of 100 great women athletes from around the world. Reading level: 4th–8th grade.

Johnson, William Oscar. *The Olympics*. Birmingham, AL: Oxmoor House, 1992. 224 pp. This oversized book brings to life the athletes and historic events associated with the Olympics. Reading level: 8th grade–Adult.

Knight, Theodore. *The Olympic Games*. San Diego, CA: Lucent Books, 1991. 112 pp. Superb resource on the history, records, politics, and achievements of the Olympics. Reading level: 4th–8th grade.

Littlefield, Bill. Champions: *Stories of Ten Remarkable Athletes*. Boston, MA: Little, Brown and Co. 1993. 132 pp. Highly recommended for the detailed accounts of ten athletes, such as Pele, the soccer player; Roberto Clemente, baseball player; and Susan Butcher, dogsled racer; who demonstrated tremendous courage and will power to excel. Beautifully illustrated paintings by Bernie Fuchs. Reading level: 4th–8th grade.

Maid, Amy and Roger Wallace. *Not Just Schoolwork*. N.L. Assoc., Inc., 1987. This excellent resource provides journal and story ideas for teachers.

Nelson, Rebecca and Marie J. MacNee *The Olympic Factbook*. Detroit, MI: Facts on File, 1996. 855pp. Published with contributions from the U.S. Olympic Committee, this is an extraordinary manual covering the Summer events for 1996 including the history of the events, the records, and the hopefuls for 1996. Reading level: 6th–Adult.

O'Connor, Jim. *Comeback! Four True Stories.* New York: Random House, 1992. 48 pp. A part of the "Step into Reading" Series, this book includes stories about Wilma Ruldoph, Jim Hunter, Bart Ontario Science Centre. Sportworks. Toronto, Ontario: The Centennial Centre of Science and Technology. 1989. 96pp. Invaluable resource for science or physical education teachers presenting over 50 science experiments related to sports. Reading level: 4th–8th grade.

Snelling, Lauraine. *High Hurdles.* Minneapolis, MN: Bethany House Publishers, 1995. 155 pp. Fictional story about a thirteen-year old girl named DJ who dreams of being in the show jumping equestrian event in the Olympics. Reading level: 4th–8th grade.

Tillman, Kenneth G. and Patricia Rizzo Toner. *You'll Never Guess What We Did in Gym Today!* New York: Parker, 1987.

Woolum, Janet. *Outstanding Women Athletes.* Phoenix, AZ: Oryx Press, 1992. 279 pp. Offers biographical information on prominent women in a wide range of sports, a selected bibliography, and a directory of organizations that promote participation in women's sports. Reading level: 5th–8th grade.

Young, Mark. *The Guinness Book of Sports Records 1994-1995.* New York: Guinness Publishing, 1994. 250 pp. Offers updated statistics and records for over 70 sports. Reading level: 3rd grade–Adult.

Olympic Information Available on the World Wide Web.

Atlanta Committee for the Olympic Games
http://www.atlanta.olympic.org   This is the official Web site for the 1996 Olympic Games. It contains event schedules, ticket and travel information, and other useful data.

Atlanta Journal-Constitution 1996 Olympics Report
http://www.ajc.com   Olympic news updates, Olympics Weekly, Olympic Guide, and visitor information about Atlanta.

Dave's 1996 Olympic Web Site Hotlist
http://www.com-stock.com/dave   This offers links to a wide variety of Web sites that provide information about the 1996 Atlanta Games.

Sports Illustrated
http://www.pathfinder.com/si   Contains Olympic schedules, current news, and event coverage.

USA TODAY Sports
http://www.usatoday.com/sports/other/sooly.htm   This national newspaper offers daily updates on Olympic news, events and athletes.

Index